THE BATTLES FOR RICHMOND, 1862

CIVIL WAR SERIES

TEXT BY WILLIAM J. MILLER

Maps by George Skoch

Thanks to Michael Andrus, Robert Krick, and the interpretive staff at Richmond National Battlefield Park.

Published by Eastern National, copyright 1996.

Eastern National provides quality educational products and services to America's national parks and other public trusts.

Front cover: *Desperate Valor* by Dale Gallon, courtesy of Dale Gallon Historical Art Gallery, Gettysburg, PA.

Back cover: *Malvern Hill* by Don Stivers.

Printed on recycled paper.

To order additional titles in the Civil War Series or other park-related items, please call 1-800-821-2903, or visit our online store at www.eParks.com.

THE BATTLES FOR RICHMOND, 1862

*I*t was mid-May 1862 when Jefferson Davis of Mississippi came to the great crisis of his life. Davis had devoted his existence to serving his home state and his country, and that path had led him to the presidency of the Confederate States of America. Yet a lifetime of labor and commitment to principle had brought him no repose to enjoy his accomplishments. Indeed, in that spring of 1862, he found himself standing not on a pinnacle of power but a precipice of defeat. His world appeared to be on the verge of collapse, and he was virtually powerless to stop it.

By mid-May 1862, newspaper editors across the divided nation openly declared that Davis's battered Southern Confederacy was doomed. Confederate troops had triumphed in the war's first major battle, at Manassas, Virginia, in July 1861, but since then the litany of Southern defeats was long and almost unbroken: in Tennessee at Forts Henry and Donelson and at Shiloh, in Arkansas at Pea Ridge, in North Carolina at Hatteras, Roanoke Island, and New Berne, in Georgia at Fort Pulaski, and in Louisiana, where New Orleans, the South's largest and wealthiest city, lived under Federal martial law. In Virginia, an army of more than 100,000 Federals, the largest army in American history to that point stood just 25 miles from Richmond—the Confederacy's capital and its leading industrial city. Richmond's defense depended upon an army of 60,000 inexperienced and poorly organized troops. Few disagreed when on May 12, the *New York Times* declared: "In no representation of the rebel cause is there a gleam of hope."

It was in an atmosphere of desperation, therefore, that President Davis convened his Confederate cabinet in mid-May. Davis asked these men to consider the Confederacy's last ditch—what should

WITH 38,000 RESIDENTS IN 1860, RICHMOND RANKED THIRD IN POPULATION AMONG ALL SOUTHERN CITIES. THE CITY'S CAPACITY FOR PRODUCING MANUFACTURED GOODS, PARTICULARLY IRON, HELPED CONVINCE THE CONFEDERATE GOVERNMENT TO RELOCATE THE CAPITAL HERE. OVERCROWDING AND SHORTAGES SOON BELIED THIS IDYLLIC PICTURE OF CONFEDERATE RICHMOND.

(LC)

they do if Richmond were lost? Present at the meeting was Davis's military adviser, General Robert E. Lee. Lee was a Virginian. His mother's father had been one of the wealthiest landowners in the state. Lee's own father had led troops under Washington in the Revolution and had served as governor of Virginia. The fate of Richmond was therefore of more than professional concern to the 55-year-old soldier. He courteously advised the president that if Richmond fell, the next militarily defensible line in Virginia would be along the Staunton River, about 100 miles southwest of the city. Then, much to the surprise of the men present, Lee added a personal opinion, almost a plea: "But," he said, in a firm voice, "Richmond must not be given up"; tears welled in his eyes, "it shall not be given up!"

Coming after months of Southern defeats, Robert E. Lee's emotional declaration stands as a watershed in the early history of the Confederacy. Jefferson Davis's dedication had been powerful and unwavering in the first year of the war, but the South's oft-defeated generals had been at best merely competent. Lee's ardor on behalf of Richmond and all it symbolized suggested that perhaps he was a different kind of soldier. Here was a military man who seemed touched by powerful, even passionate determination. Within six weeks, the courtly Virginian would reveal for all to see another side of his character—a boldness and decisiveness that would very suddenly turn defeat into victory and completely reverse the course of the war.

Before Davis appointed Lee to be his adviser in mid-March 1862, all of the military problems of defending Confederate Virginia were laid at the feet of General Joseph E. Johnston. Small, trim, and meticulously neat, the 55-year-old Virginian was a career soldier. Though popular with his men, Johnston was proud to the point of perceiving slights where none existed. After the Confederate victory at the Battle of Manassas on July 21, 1861, a victory that owed much to Johnston's leadership, the general seemed jealous of credit going to anyone but him. Relations between Johnston and his civilian superiors in Richmond were stormy, and the general and President Davis seemed to be as much private adversaries as public allies.

Perhaps worse than his strained relations with Davis was the condition of Johnston's army. In April and May of 1861, a great many Southerners had enlisted to fight for one year. Those enlistments would expire in the spring of 1862 with the war far from won and as the Confederacy was to face its greatest crisis. The Confederate Congress passed a conscription act—the first in American history —which drafted recruits and forced current soldiers to remain in the ranks. The veterans were outraged, and morale and discipline declined.

Greatest of all of Johnston's concerns, however, was the position of his army. His troops had spent the winter in camps around Manassas, a railroad town about 30 miles west of Washington. By spring 1862, Johnston could marshal only about 42,000 men and worried that the

GENERAL
JOSEPH E. JOHNSTON
(USAMHI)

3

Northerners would discover his weakness. In February, Johnston conferred with Davis about pulling the army back from its advanced position to a defensive line nearer the capital. The only results of the seven-hour meeting were confusion and hard feelings. Davis later said he had directed Johnston to stay at Manassas as long as possible. Johnston believed he had discretionary power to withdraw whenever he deemed it prudent. The misunderstanding led to a widening of the breach between the general and the president, and as the battle for Richmond loomed in the spring of 1862, the two men remained more than ever disaffected partners in an unsteady alliance to save the Confederacy.

But by the spring of 1862, the Federal army had grown so powerful that the Confederates' plans seemed almost unimportant. The size of the Federal Army of the Potomac—more than 200,000 men —led many in Washington to think it virtually invincible. The great army's commander, Major General George B. McClellan, "The Young Napoleon," as the newspapers called him, was already the idol of his army and had many admirers among the people of the North and the powerful of Washington. If he took Richmond and ended the war, McClellan would be hailed as the greatest hero of the age, and he knew it.

The mustachioed young general—he was only 35—was the product of Philadelphia society. Graduated second in his class at West Point, he had distinguished himself as a military engineer in the war with Mexico and after. His superiors saw him as a rising star and cultivated his professional growth, but despite his many accomplishments, the young captain grew impatient with the slow promotion and low pay in the army. He resigned in 1857 to begin a promising and initially highly successful career as a railroad executive. When the war came in 1861, George McClellan was considered brilliant and popular and had been extraordinarily successful in the army and in private business. It was logical that Northern leaders looked to him to lead troops when the war broke out. Just three months after the beginning of hostilities, President

Abraham Lincoln called McClellan to Washington to sort out the confusion in the wake of the debacle at Manassas.

McClellan arrived in Washington in late July 1861 to find a disorganized and defeated army of about 52,000 and a city full of politicians near panic. Radiating competence and self-assurance, the general soon calmed the hysteria. Within three months, he had 134,000 soldiers trained and armed around Washington, and the army was growing by the week. The Northern states demonstrated their tremendous power and commitment to the cause by sending tens of thousands of recruits and hundreds of cannon to McClellan so that by the end of December 1861 the Army of the Potomac numbered 220,000 men and more than 500 cannon —a force many times greater than the largest army in the nation's short history.

President Abraham Lincoln watched this impressive performance by the young man and was inspired to give him even greater authority in directing the Union war effort. On November 1, 1861, Lincoln appointed McClellan to command "the whole army" of the United States. McClellan would be responsible not just for the actions of his own army, but for the movements of all the Federal armies in all the theaters of war. Lincoln expressed concern that perhaps the job was too big for his young general. McClellan's self-assurance seems to have had no bounds. He told the president, "I can do it all."

But "Little Mac" had considerably less confidence in others. Washington politicians in general and the president in particular appear to have merited neither his admiration nor his trust. McClellan was a conservative Democrat in a town where liberal Republicans held power. Many

Republicans wished to replace him at the head of the army with one of their own. That Lincoln was not among these seems not to have mattered to McClellan, for he clearly did not respect Lincoln as a man or a leader. The general was negligent in paying to Lincoln the courtesy traditionally due the president and on occasion referred privately to the commander in chief as a "gorilla." Matters of decorum aside, McClellan took pains to conceal from Lincoln and Secretary of War Edwin M. Stanton his plans for the spring campaigns. The general was understandably concerned about security, but by showing such disrespect for his civilian collaborators, who were also his legal superiors, he almost certainly undermined their confidence in him.

McCLELLAN'S HEADQUARTERS NEAR YORKTOWN.

(LC)

As the winter weeks passed and the army grew, so did the outcry for McClellan to do something. Unfazed, McClellan developed with great deliberation his plan for a campaign he believed would end the war. His national strategy called for a simultaneous movement by Federal armies upon the heart of the Confederacy. According to his plan, Nashville would fall, followed by all of

Tennessee; Federal armies would secure Missouri and the Mississippi River, New Orleans, the Carolina coasts and, most important, Richmond. He thought the outcome by no means certain if the job was undertaken hastily. "I have ever regarded our true policy as being that of fully preparing ourselves, and then seeking for the most decisive result," he wrote the president. In other words, he wished no half measures; he wished to make one grand, overwhelming, and irresistible effort.

By December 1861, McClellan, had sketched out a plan for a campaign in Virginia—a movement he would lead himself. His "Urbanna Plan" called for the movement of the Army of the Potomac from Washington, D.C., by water down the Chesapeake Bay to the river town of Urbanna, Virginia, on the Rappahannock River, 60 miles from Richmond. From Urbanna, the army would advance rapidly overland to Richmond. Despite his reservations, Lincoln approved McClellan's plan of campaign as long as the general would leave Washington secure in the army's absence.

But in early March, two events occurred that completely altered the strategic picture in Virginia. A bright, clear Saturday, March 8, 1862, became the most dismal day in the 86-year history of the United States Navy. The Confederate ironclad *Virginia*, a vessel unlike any warship ever seen afloat, steamed out of its home berth at the Gosport Navy Yard near Norfolk, Virginia, and attacked Federal ships in Hampton Roads. Three hours later, two Federal frigates lay destroyed and 250 U.S. sailors and marines were dead or wounded. The *Virginia*, scarcely hurt, would be ready to fight again the next day. Navy pride, however, would be redeemed on that morrow by the just-arrived little gunboat USS *Monitor*. The historic clash between these two ironclads on March 9 ended in a draw, and the *Virginia* retired to her moorings in the Elizabeth River to refit and prepare for another day.

It was the contemplation of another day like March 8 that dominated the thinking of Federal strategists for more than two crucial months that spring. Norfolk and its docks lay at the mouth of the James River. About 100 tortuous miles upstream sat Richmond on high bluffs overlooking the brown waters of the river that had helped make the city the South's leading manufacturing center. If the combined forces of the Federal army and navy sought a doorway to Richmond, the James was an obvious and very desirable option—but not so long as the fearsome *Virginia* guarded the entrance to Richmond's river. McClellan had to look elsewhere for a route to the Confederate capital. Simply by its existence, therefore, this single Confederate ship—the

ugly, turtlelike craft with balky engines—dominated the early phases of the Federal conduct of the campaign.

The second pivotal event that March came when Johnston exercised what he believed was his authority to withdraw from Manassas. His army moved toward Gordonsville in central Virginia to a more secure position behind the Rappahannock and Rapidan Rivers, leaving or destroying more than 750,000 tons of food, thousands of tons of clothing and supplies, and dozens of heavy artillery guns at Centreville and Manassas. Davis was angry, not just that Johnston had evacuated his position but that he had been so hasty as to abandon food, supplies, and weapons precious to the Confederacy.

The Confederates now sat on a railroad just several hours' ride from Richmond. McClellan realized that his cherished scheme of an amphibious sweep around the enemy's flank would no longer work as he had hoped. "When Manassas had been abandoned by the enemy," he wrote after the war, "and he had withdrawn behind the Rapidan, the Urbanna movement lost much of its promise, as the enemy was now in position to reach Richmond before we could do so." In the game of chess for control of Virginia, Johnston had sidestepped the expected Federal offensive yet remained in a fine position to react promptly to any Federal movement on Richmond. Johnston waited for McClellan's next move.

McClellan, his generals, and the president finally agreed to proceed with plans for the now less-lustrous amphibi-

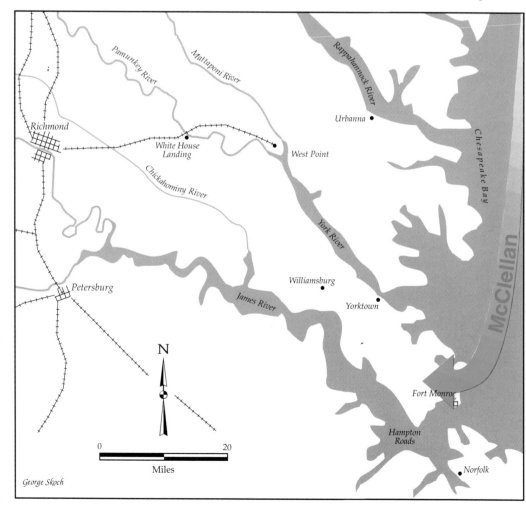

George Skoch

THE PENINSULA CAMPAIGN BEGINS General McClellan's original plan called for a landing at Urbanna on the Rappahannock River. From there the Army of the Potomac would march overland toward Richmond. The Urbanna Plan was quickly discarded, however, when General Joseph Johnston abandoned his position near Manassas Junction and ordered the Confederate army closer to Richmond. The move forced McClellan to revise his operation. He decided to land the Union army at Fort Monroe and march up the peninsula between the York and James Rivers toward Richmond.

ous route down the Chesapeake Bay. The Federal commander planned to move to the Virginia peninsula formed by the York River on the north and the James River on the south. From Fort Monroe at the tip of the Peninsula, McClellan intended, with the help of the U.S. Navy, to force the small Confederate garrisons at Yorktown and Gloucester Point on the York River to retreat, opening the York to Federal shipping. McClellan then hoped to move his army by water up the river to West Point at the confluence of the Pamunkey and Mattaponi Rivers. From West Point, McClellan hoped to move quickly westward along the Richmond & York River Railroad to the capital of the Confederacy just 30 miles away.

McClellan was confident of victory, for his army seemed irresistible. His host of 155,000 was the largest armed force in American history to that point—almost four times larger than the entire American army in the Mexican War and seven times bigger than the largest force McClellan had ever commanded in the field. "The Young Napoleon's" move to capture Richmond was nothing less than the most enormous and complicated military opera-

tion in U.S. history and would remain so even into the twentieth century.

On March 17, the first of McClellan's troops departed aboard ship from Alexandria, Virginia, and steamed down the Potomac. The Federals had assembled a fleet of 389 steamers and schooners to transport the army. For three weeks the waters of the Potomac churned with activity as the invaders shipped vast numbers of men, animals, cannons, and wagons southward. McClellan boarded a steamer at Alexandria on April 1 and cast off for his rendezvous with destiny. The general was deeply happy to leave behind the politics of Washington and join the army in the field. "Officially speaking," he wrote to his wife, "I feel very glad to get away from that sink of iniquity."

But McClellan's troubles with Washington were just beginning. Lincoln had stipulated that McClellan must leave about 40,000 men behind to ensure that Washington was "entirely secure." McClellan reported he had left more than 55,000 men behind, but the War Department learned that only about 19,000 men remained to defend the capital and that 35,000 of the troops McClellan

AFTER SUCCESSFULLY COMPLETING THE JOURNEY FROM ALEXANDRIA BY SHIP, UNION SOLDIERS LANDED AT HAMPTON.

(LC)

counted as defenders of Washington were 100 miles away in the Shenandoah Valley. The War Department immediately withheld 35,000 men slated to join McClellan, infuriating the general, who called the order "the most infamous thing that history has recorded."

McClellan pushed onward from Fort Monroe toward the Confederate fortifications at the historic old town of Yorktown. Admiral Louis M. Goldsborough informed McClellan that the U.S. Navy could not assist him in forcing past Yorktown, so the general planned to outmaneuver the position and force the Confederate garrison to withdraw.

No sooner had McClellan's divisions moved forward than they encountered the unexpected. The roads, which McClellan had told the president were dry and sandy and passable in all seasons, were in reality small and muddy. The continuous passage of heavy wagons, artillery pieces, and thousands of men and horses churned the roads into morasses of mud. The "rapid marches" that had composed a significant component of McClellan's strategy, proved impossible, and every march became a slow essay in exhaustion for the men of the ranks.

Even more fatal to McClellan's intentions was the discovery that his maps were grossly inaccurate. The general was stunned to learn that the Warwick River lay athwart his intended path and that the Confederates had constructed elaborate fortifications on the west bank from Yorktown to the James. McClellan's chief engineer declared that the line of works was "certainly one of the most extensive known to modern times."

More distressing to McClellan were

reports that the Confederates were present in great strength across the Warwick. Federal officers reported seeing long columns of Southern troops moving about and clearly hearing the creaking and groaning of wagons and artillery on roads behind the Confederate front lines. McClellan's intelligence operatives reported that the Confederate garrison along the Warwick numbered perhaps 100,000, and the general decided that formidable works manned by so many defenders were impregnable to assaults by infantry. An engineer by training, McClellan had studied siege warfare and had brought with him dozens of enormous artillery pieces—guns so large they could hurl explosive shells weighing 200 pounds more than three miles. The Federal commander knew that preparations for a siege would take many days, perhaps weeks, but he reasoned that even though he would be losing time, he would be saving lives.

The Warwick River defenses were not nearly as strong as he thought they were. John B. Magruder commanded perhaps 13,000 Southern men in Yorktown and along the Warwick, but he made the most of them. A career soldier known among his brother officers of the old army for his panache and theatrical flair, Magruder staged an elaborate show for McClellan's scouts. Throughout April 4,

ALFRED R. WAUD'S DEPICTION OF MCCLELLAN RECONNOITERING THE LINES AT YORKTOWN.

(LC)

9

HIGH-TECH WARFARE, 1862

Of all the advanced implements of war used on the Peninsula, none better represented the terrible destructive potential of modern technology than Mr. Wilson Ager's volley gun.

The high stakes of the Peninsula campaign — the fate of Richmond and with it, perhaps, the Confederacy—drove leaders on both sides to seek every advantage in battle, including using some of the latest military technology on land, sea, and in the air.

Probably the most famous new weapon of the Peninsula campaign was the ironclad warship. European naval engineers had experimented with ironclad ships, but not until the spectacular events of March 1862 in Hampton Roads, Virginia, did ironclads prove wooden warships were obsolete. The turtlelike CSS *Virginia* and the new USS *Monitor*, a "ridiculous-looking" vessel of radical design that one soldier thought looked like a cheesebox on a giant pumpkin seed, battled to an inconclusive draw on March 9, 1862, off the tip of the Peninsula. Their duel marked a turning point in naval history and revealed to the world that henceforth iron warships would rule the waves.

Hot-air and gas balloons were not new in 1862, but technical problems had limited the military uses of airships. An energetic 29-year-old New Hampshire native named Thaddeus Lowe convinced both McClellan and President Lincoln that balloons could be of great value in aerial reconnaissance. Though Lowe had built and ascended in his first balloon just four years earlier, Lincoln made him chief of army aeronautics in August 1861, and the young Yankee went to work creating a fleet of balloons, the most famous of which was the Intrepid. He worked out a way to get portable gas generators into the field and took them to the Peninsula, where he immediately proved valuable. He and army officers made almost daily ascents to gather intelligence on Confederate positions, and Lowe became the first person to communicate with the ground from a balloon via telegraph. Brigadier General Fitz John Porter went aloft to observe Confederate activity at Yorktown when a tether line failed and winds bore the balloon westward over enemy lines. Southern marksmen tried to shoot the airship down, but the wind shifted and took Porter back to his blue-suited friends.

Captain E. P. Alexander had charge of the Confederate aerial reconnaissance program, which enjoyed few of the advantages of its Northern counterpart. Lacking portable inflation machinery, the Confederates had to fill the balloon at the Richmond Gas Works, transport it by rail to the James River and tether it to a boat—the CSS *Teaser*—a bargelike vessel that was arguably the first aircraft carrier.

American businessmen had been using railroads for decades before the Civil War, but not until the Peninsula campaign did military men see what the iron roads could do for armies actively engaged in field operations. McClellan made the Peninsula's one rail line—the small Richmond & York River Railroad—a linchpin of his strategy. The enormous Army of the Potomac consumed 600 tons of food, forage, and supplies each day, every pound of which had to come hundreds of miles from the North. Ships carried the food and supplies to the Peninsula, and wagons took the matériel into the army's camps. Using the railroad lifted a tremendous burden from McClellan's supply officers because it could quickly move tons of rations to within a few miles of the army's camps on the Chickahominy. So dependent did the Federals become on the rails that one Union general stated that the Army of the Potomac could not survive more than 10 miles from a railroad.

The Confederates used the railroads most profitably by moving men. Five railroads

Magruder ran his troops to and fro behind the lines, across clearings and along roads, always with a view toward being seen by the enemy. The newly arrived Federals counted many thousands of gray-clad soldiers and reported to headquarters that the Confederates seemed to be receiving heavy reinforcements. Magruder's bluff helped convince McClellan that the Confederates were much too strong to be dislodged quickly, and the Federals resigned themselves to bringing up their heavy guns.

Johnston moved his army to the Peninsula to reinforce Magruder at Yorktown, where Johnston assumed command. Though Magruder's extensive preparations and imaginative theatrics had halted the Federal advance—and the commanding general fully appreciated Magruder's "resolute and judicious" efforts to buy the Confederacy precious time— Johnston did not like what he saw along the Warwick. He was not as impressed converged at Richmond, and the Southerners brought troops over the rails from North Carolina and other parts of the Confederacy to defend the capital. Robert E. Lee's plan for a countermovement against McClellan late in June probably would not have been possible had not he been able to use the Virginia Central Railroad to move "Stonewall" Jackson's men rapidly from the Shenandoah Valley to Richmond.

By far the most innovative use of railroads in the campaign sprang from Lee's fertile mind early in June. Lee directed Confederate military engineers to work with the C.S. Navy in mounting a powerful Brooke Naval Rifle on a flatcar. This gun could accurately fire 32-pound explosive shells more than a mile. The Confederates mounted the 7,200-pound cannon behind a sloping wall of iron affixed to the flatcar and rolled the armored railroad gun —among the first in history— into action at the Battle of Savage's Station, June 29, 1862. The gun accounted for some Federal casualties, but its chief accomplishment seems to have been scaring Federal soldiers, many of them patients in a nearby field hospital, with the screech of its large shells.

More controversial were the shells deployed by Confederate Brigadier General Gabriel J. Rains. Just before the Confederate evacuation of Yorktown, Rains ordered his men to bury large artillery shells a few inches underground around wells and in roadways and rig the devices to explode when stepped on. Officers in both armies were still chivalric enough to denounce the land mines as barbaric, and angry Federals used Confederate prisoners to find and excavate the "infernal machines."

Of all the advanced implements of war used on the Peninsula, none better represented the terrible destructive potential of modern technology than Wilson Ager's volley gun. Like the more famous Gatling gun, this rapid-fire weapon was a direct ancestor of the modern machine gun and spat scores of bullets per minute. Soldiers called it a "coffee mill gun" because gunners loaded ammunition into a hopper and turned a hand crank to fire the weapon. Several Ager guns saw action at Gaines's Mill, where soldiers reported hearing "the quick popping of a rapid firing gun" above the din of battle. The Agers had little effect at Gaines's Mill but had far more significant influence in inspiring inventors to create evermore devastating weapons and usher in the age of quick and efficient wholesale destruction that is the hallmark of modern technological warfare.

with the fortifications as was McClellan. "The works had been constructed under the direction of engineers without experience in war or engineering," he later wrote, and there was a dangerous gap in the defenses near Yorktown. He felt certain a determined assault would pierce the Warwick line.

Perhaps the more compelling reason behind Johnston's disdain for the Confederate works on the lower Peninsula was that they did not fit in with his plans, and he did not wish to hold them. Johnston believed that however strong were the entrenchments themselves along the Warwick, "they would not enable us to defeat McClellan." He was convinced that "we could do no more on the Peninsula than delay General McClellan's progress toward Richmond." A Federal breakthrough along the Warwick was inevitable, he thought, and because the flanks of Magruder's line were vulnerable the position was doomed. If the

Federal navy wrested control of either the York or the James and passed gunboats upstream beyond the Confederate flank, Johnston's position would be untenable. The general wished to withdraw from Yorktown immediately to take up a defensive position closer to the capital. President Davis and Robert E. Lee also understood that the rivers were the key to the defenses of Yorktown but saw that Johnston could buy valuable time for the Confederacy by keeping McClellan at bay on the Warwick. The longer the Federals sat stymied, the more time Davis and Lee would have to gather troops from across the Confederacy and move them to Richmond to confront McClellan. Johnston, Davis, and Lee met on April 14 in Richmond but could come to no agreement. Lee argued vehemently with his old friend (Lee and Johnston had been classmates at West Point) that time was of the essence. Johnston thought holding the Warwick was a flirtation with disaster and left the meeting determined to evacuate Yorktown as soon as possible, but he did not declare as much to Davis and Lee, who assumed the army commander would hold his position until they could all discuss it again.

On the morning of April 30, McClellan wrote to his wife that preparations were almost complete for opening fire with the siege guns. "We are working like horses and will soon be ready to open. It will be a tremendous affair when we do begin, and will, I hope, make short work of it."

But the Confederates too had been working. For Johnston, the issue at Yorktown was whether he could get his army away before the Federals were ready to begin their bombardment. By May 3, Johnston and his army were about ready, and the general planned to screen his withdrawal with a bombardment from his own heavy guns. Later that day, Johnston's batteries opened on the Federal lines. "The shells from the rifled guns flew in all directions," noted one of McClellan's staff officers. The firing con-

tinued into the night, and the roar was
deafening.

Dawn at last came, "silent as death,"
according to one Federal. Far forward,
along the picket lines, the Federals crept
forward and discovered the startling news:
the Confederates were gone.

As soon as he learned of Johnston's
pullout, a jubilant McClellan ordered his
divisions forward in pursuit. Soupy roads
slowed both armies, and rain continued to
fall. Johnston kept with the head of his
column as it labored through the mud, so
not until the afternoon of May 5 did he
learn that the Federals had attacked his
rear guard at Williamsburg, eight miles
from Yorktown.

Long before the Federals had arrived
on the Peninsula, Magruder's Confederates
had built a line of earthworks just east of
the old colonial capital of Williamsburg.
The defensive line's centerpiece, Fort
Magruder, dominated the main road from
Yorktown. In the cold, rainy dawn of
May 5, Southern infantrymen and artillerymen lay in the muddy earthen ramparts
of the fort and peered eastward into the

murk. Federals of Brigadier General
Joseph Hooker's division strode through
the fog toward Fort Magruder and
immediately deployed for an attack.
Confederate artillerymen in the fort
opened an accurate fire, and Confederate
infantrymen soon joined the fight. Major
General James Longstreet, a South
Carolinian and perhaps Johnston's most
trusted lieutenant, conducted the engage-
ment in Johnston's absence and sent more
Southern brigades that came forward to
counter the persistent Hooker. The fighting shifted southwestward from Fort
Magruder, where Brigadier General
Richard H. Anderson advanced through
tangled woods to assail Hooker's left.
Longstreet eventually committed his entire
division of six brigades against Hooker's
three, and the Federals barely held
their own.

Brigadier General Philip Kearny's
division came to Hooker's relief. Certainly
one of the more colorful figures in either
army, Kearny led his men up from the
rear, flourishing his sword in his one hand
—he had lost his left arm in the Mexican

War. Kearny cantered forward on a personal reconnaissance to draw enemy fire. Two riders with him fell dead, but the general returned to his troops pleased, for the Confederates in the woods had revealed their positions. "You see, my boys, where to fire!" he shouted, and his worshipful men sprang forward with a yell. Kearny urged regiment upon regiment forward, shouting, "Men, I want you to drive those blackguards to hell at once." Anderson's Confederates fell back, and the fighting southwest of Fort Magruder settled into a stalemate.

North of the fort, however, a Federal brigade moved forward into what appeared to be a gap in the Confederate line. Brigadier General Winfield S. Hancock, a Pennsylvanian, pushed his men onward until he found himself in the Confederate rear and approaching Fort Magruder from behind. Longstreet, with all of his troops engaged with Hooker and Kearny, had no reserve with which to counter Hancock and sent an urgent appeal to Major General D. H. Hill for reinforcements. Hill sent Brigadier General Jubal A. Early and his four regiments hustling to the Confederate left. Early's Virginians and North Carolinians emerged from a forest and found themselves in the open directly before Hancock's troops. Early launched an attack, and a Federal officer on the battle line recalled that Hancock's line moved swiftly to counter it: "We halted and opened fire, and the view of it through the smoke was pitiful. They were falling everywhere; white handerchiefs were held up in token of surrender. . . . We gathered in some three hundred prisoners before dark." All told, Early had lost more than 500 men (300

from the 5th North Carolina alone) and had himself been gravely wounded.

The battle sputtered to a close in the soggy darkness, and commanders were left to count their dead, wounded, and missing. In this first pitched battle of the Peninsula campaign, the Federals spent 2,200 men in trying to smash the Confederates from behind, and the Southerners lost 1,600 soldiers in fending off the Federal attackers.

But McClellan had already undertaken a more ambitious movement aimed not at the tail of the retreating Confederate column but at its head. As his divisions had streamed through Yorktown and on to Williamsburg on May 4 and 5, McClellan went to the wharves of Yorktown to oversee the loading of 11,000 soldiers and their supplies and equipment on to steamers and barges. The general's plan was for his close friend Brigadier General William B. Franklin to lead a division up the York River, which, with the abandonment of the Confederate batteries at Yorktown and Gloucester Point, was open to Federal shipping. Franklin was to establish a landing near West Point and, if possible, strike inland at Johnston's retreating column. If all went well for the Federals, Franklin's move might be the bold stroke of the campaign —the blow that might severely hurt Johnston and, perhaps, set enough dominoes tumbling to lead to the fall of Richmond. But neither McClellan nor Franklin seemed to have the heart to deliver a crushing blow. McClellan seemed more concerned about the risks involved than the victory to be won and emphasized caution. Rather than releasing this flanking force for a daring thrust, McClellan seemed satisfied to place

Franklin on Johnston's flank and keep him there on a leash.

Franklin landed at Eltham's Landing on the Pamunkey River on the afternoon of May 6 while most of Johnston's army was still slogging along the muddy roads from Williamsburg. Instead of striking inland to intercept the enemy, Franklin adhered to the spirit of his orders and fortified the landing site. Three Confederate brigades stifled a small Federal sally the next day, ending McClellan's best opportunity yet to hit the Confederates hard away from the protection of their earthworks.

Franklin did, however, establish a beachhead, and McClellan's supply officers immediately sent heavily laden vessels up the York. For the next seven weeks, the York would be one of the busier rivers in America as craft of all types labored to supply the army as it moved toward Richmond.

The James River, to the south, would be less busy but no more placid. In the second week of May, the U.S. Navy at last got its chance to add its heavy ordnance to the contest on the Peninsula. When Johnston had evacuated Yorktown, the commander of the Confederate garrison at Norfolk withdrew his troops toward Richmond, abandoning the Gosport Navy Yard, home port of the ironclad *Virginia*. The James River was too shallow for the

McCLELLAN'S SUPERI-
OR LOGISTICAL ABILITY
MANIFESTED ITSELF
ON THE WHARVES OF
YORKTOWN WHERE HE
STOCKPILED STORES OF
AMMUNITION AND
EQUIPMENT.

(USAMHI)

ironclad to retreat toward Richmond so, reluctantly, the captain scuttled and burned his ship before dawn on May 11. It was an ignominious end for the ship that had dominated the campaign for two months.

Free at last from the shadow of its nemesis, the U.S. Navy immediately entered the waters of the James that the *Virginia* had so long denied them. Admiral Louis M. Goldsborough placed five gunboats under the command of Commander John Rodgers and ordered the squadron to push upriver to Richmond. Goldsborough told Rodgers to "shell the place into a surrender."

Davis and others in Richmond clearly understood the gravity of the situation. The president told Virginia's legislature that he intended to hold Richmond, but the statement was neither a promise nor very convincing. "There is no doubt," wrote Richmond newspaperman Edward Pollard, "that about this time the authorities of the Confederate States had nigh despaired of the safety of Richmond." While their leaders spoke of brave deeds and the need for courage, the people of Richmond watched as the Confederate government began packing up. "They added to the public alarm by preparations to remove the archives," Pollard wrote. "They ran off their wives and children to the country." Davis himself had sent his wife and children to safety in North Carolina. "As the clouds grow darker and when one after another of those who were trusted are detected in secret hostility," he wrote, she must try to "be of good cheer and continue to hope that God will in due time deliver us from the hands of our enemies and 'sanctify

to us our deepest distress.'"

Just eight miles south of Richmond, hundreds of Southern soldiers, sailors, marines, militiamen, and civilians labored to obstruct the James River and thus seal off the greatest immediate threat to the capital. For weeks, men had worked to finish a fort high atop the 90-foot-high Drewry's Bluff. Work on the defenses continued through the night of May 14, when the Southerners sank cribs full of stones and small ships to close off the river's channel.

Rodgers's squadron steamed around a sharp bend at 7:30 A.M. on May 15 and came under fire from the guns on the bluff (the Federals referred to the earthworks on the heights as Fort Darling). Rodgers boldy steered his flagship, the ironclad USS *Galena*, to within 600 yards of the fort. The other gunboats, the *Monitor*, *Aroostook*, *Port Royal*, and *Naugatuck*, anchored behind the *Galena* and returned fire. The Southern artillerymen concentrated their fire on the *Galena*, and the riflemen along the river's edge sniped at the Federal gun crews. More than three hours after the fight had begun, Rodgers decided he could do no more. "It became evident after a time that it was useless for us to contend against the terrific strength & accuracy of their fire," wrote an officer on the *Monitor*. The *Galena*, having expended 360 rounds, was nearly out of ammunition and was on fire. Rodgers ordered his ships to retire downriver.

The *Galena* had been hit 45 times. One onlooker thought her iron sides had offered "no more resistance than an eggshell." An officer of the *Monitor* was stunned by what he saw belowdecks on the *Galena*, where 13 men had been

killed and 11 others wounded—"she looked like a slaughterhouse. . . . Here was a body with the head, one arm & part of the breast torn off by a bursting shell—another with the top of his head taken off the brains still steaming on the deck, partly across him lay one with both legs taken off at the hips & at a little dis-

tance was another completely disemboweled. The sides & ceiling overhead, the ropes & guns were spattered with blood & brains & lumps of flesh while the decks were covered with large pools of half coagulated blood & strewn with portions of skulls, fragments of shells, arms legs, hands, pieces of flesh & iron, splinters of wood & broken weapons mixed in one confused, horrible mass."

Richmond celebrated the repulse of Rodgers as the first good news in weeks. The James River route to the city had again been denied to the Federal navy at the cost of just seven Confederates killed and eight wounded.

With proper management and good

17

fortune, any of the three Federal thrusts in the first half of May—those at Williamsburg, Eltham's Landing, and Drewry's Bluff—might have proved fatal to Johnston's defense of Richmond. But the Federals had been neither adroit nor lucky, and the Confederates drew confidence from the Federal failures as the initiative in the campaign shifted slightly toward Johnston. McClellan seemed willing to let it pass, for after the setback at Eltham's Landing, he had ceased pursuing Johnston with vigor and moved haltingly toward the Pamunkey River, where his quartermasters were accumulating vast supplies.

On May 16, McClellan established his base of supply at White House Landing, where the Richmond & York River Railroad crossed the Pamunkey. Just

a few miles west of White House lay Johnston's army, where it had been resting undisturbed for more than a week. McClellan expected a climactic battle within days near the Chickahominy River, but he admitted he could not discern what Johnston was up to. "I don't yet know what to make of the rebels," he confided to his wife. "I do not see how they can possibly abandon Virginia and Richmond without a battle."

Johnston did not intend to give up Richmond without a battle, but he wished only to fight where and when it would favor his outnumbered army. The Confederates stood with their backs to the Chickahominy River, a shallow but broad, swampy morass prone to severe flooding. Johnston decided he wished this obstacle between him and the enemy rather than between his army and Richmond. On May 16, Johnston crossed the army to the south bank of the Chickahominy and took up positions west of the crossroads of Seven Pines.

Despite having made his third retrograde movement in the first three weeks of the month, Johnston was thinking offensively. He knew he would have to fight McClellan soon, but he wished to do so under the most advantageous circumstances possible. The Confederate commander believed that if he soundly defeated McClellan far from his safe haven at Fort Monroe, the Southerners could vigorously pursue the broken Federals and destroy the Army of the Potomac. "If the Federal army should be defeated a hundred miles away from its place of refuge, Fort Monroe," he wrote, "it could not escape destruction. This was undoubtedly our best hope." Contemplating this scenario, Johnston waited west of Seven

Pines and watched for an opportunity to strike.

McClellan now had a serious strategic problem before him, and he knew that how he resolved that problem would affect every decision he would make for the rest of the campaign. The Federal commander was having trouble feeding his enormous army. He discovered that his 3,000 wagons, working in tandem with the railroad, were just barely adequate to satisfy the daily requirements of his 115,000 men and 25,000 horses and mules. The thought that he might not be able to supply his army by wagon alone, particularly in rainy weather over muddy roads, understandably made McClellan reluctant to leave the railroad. Logistically, the railroad offered McClellan a great advantage in moving supplies to his troops, but to capitalize on this advantage, he had to hold both banks of the Chickahominy. Strategically, it would have been better to have consolidated the army all on one side of the river so neither wing would be isolated from the other. The principles of strategy and logistics were thus working against each other in McClellan's approach to Richmond. Opting to resolve supply problems first, even at the expense of creating strategic problems, McClellan followed Johnston across the Chickahominy with part of his force.

On May 17, after McClellan had established his base at White House, he received welcome news from the War Department. Irvin McDowell's 30,000 troops, then at Falmouth on the Rappahannock River, would march overland and join McClellan in his operations on Richmond. McClellan was pleased indeed to have these long-awaited reinforcements, but he was correspondingly outraged when a week later the War

Department suspended the order and sent McDowell instead to the Shenandoah Valley. Confederate Major General Thomas J. "Stonewall" Jackson's fast-marching troops had defeated one Federal force in the Valley, attacked another, and seemed capable of crossing the Potomac River and threatening Washington. Jackson's hyperactive campaign in the Valley—in which his men would march more than 600 miles and fight five engagements—was part of a scheme developed by Jackson and Robert E. Lee to divide Federal attention. Jackson's force was relatively small—never more than 17,000 men—but the two generals hoped that by swift forced marches and

THE PRESENCE OF UNION SOLDIERS ON THE PENINSULA REPRESENTED THE POSSIBILITY OF FREEDOM FOR THOUSANDS OF SLAVES, MANY OF WHOM RAN AWAY FROM THEIR MASTERS AND SERVED AS LABORERS IN THE UNION ARMY, INCLUDING THIS GROUP OF MEN AT WHITE HOUSE LANDING.

(USAMHI)

surprise attacks Jackson's little army could raise havoc with the Federals in the Valley and thereby create in the minds of strategists in Washington the impression of a serious crisis. Lee hoped Washington would try to subdue Jackson by diverting troops from McClellan, thereby decreasing Federal pressure on Richmond. The Federal War Department unknowingly complied with Lee's wishes and ordered McDowell westward to help corral Jackson. McClellan saw the Lee-Jackson scheme for what it was—a diversion—and he complained bitterly to Washington about sending troops to the Valley on a wild goose chase, but to no avail; he would have to do without McDowell for a while longer.

On his own, with no prospect of reinforcement any time soon, McClellan tried to sort out the strategic situation before him in the final week of May. Johnston lay behind fortifications west of Seven Pines. To get at him, McClellan would have to cross the Chickahominy in sufficient force to defeat Johnston yet leave a strong force north of the Chickahominy to protect the railroad. In

looking for his next move, McClellan's gaze turned to a gathering Confederate force north of the river near the village of Hanover Court House. McClellan saw that advancing on Johnston south of the river would place these Confederates on his flank, where it might prove troublesome, so the Federal commander decided to eliminate it before he turned his full attention to Johnston.

In the predawn hours of May 27, a Federal column commanded by Brigadier General Fitz John Porter moved north-westward through a rain storm toward Hanover Court House. Porter surprised a Confederate brigade commanded by former U.S. congressman Lawrence O'B. Branch, but the Southerners, mostly North Carolinians, fought bravely against more than twice their number. The ugly little fight sprawled through the woods and farm fields south of Hanover Court House for several hours before Branch withdrew his battered regiments toward Richmond. The Southerners had lost more than 750 men and the Federals 355, but McClellan had accomplished his objective and could now attend to Johnston.

But Johnston had already been studying McClellan's positions, and he saw that for all the Northerner's deliberations and meticulous planning, McClellan had made a careless error. While retaining most of his army north of the Chickahominy, the Federal commander had sent just two corps—the Fourth and the Third—across to the south bank. The Third Corps, under Brigadier General Samuel P. Heintzelman, remained in a reserve position close to the river while Brigadier General Erasmus D. Keyes's Fourth Corps advanced to the Seven Pines intersection, nine miles from Richmond.

MAJOR GENERAL
THOMAS J.
"STONEWALL" JACKSON

(LC)

This single corps of 17,000 men confronted the majority of the 63,000 men Johnston had at his disposal. Neither Keyes nor McClellan seem to have realized the extreme danger of the Fourth Corps's position, separated as it was from most of the army with only one bridge linking the wings across the Chickahominy. Even worse was that Keyes had pushed his weakest division, Brigadier General Silas Casey's 6,000 men, the smallest and least experienced division in the army, farthest forward to hold the most advanced position in McClellan's army—a line of earthworks just west of Seven Pines. In advancing on Johnston, McClellan had arguably put his worst foot forward.

Johnston had been looking for an opportunity to attack McClellan on favorable terms, and his numerical superiority south of the Chickahominy gave him the advantage he sought. Johnston decided to attack the Fourth Corps at Seven Pines and met with General Longstreet on the afternoon of May 30 to complete a plan. Johnston's design was not complicated. Two strong columns, one of six brigades under Longstreet and the other of four brigades under D. H. Hill, would converge via separate roads on the Fourth

Corps at Seven Pines. A third column of three brigades under Major General Benjamin Huger was to support Hill's right (the far Confederate right). G. W. Smith's division, temporarily under Brigadier General W. H. C. Whiting, was to follow Longstreet's column to add support as needed. If all went well, the Fourth Corps would be crushed and the Third Corps would be pinned against the Chickahominy and overwhelmed.

But three factors conspired to complicate the attack. The first was James Longstreet, who, without informing Johnston, decided to drastically alter the plan. For reasons he never satisfactorily explained, Longstreet chose to forsake his assigned attack route on the Nine Mile Road and move his column to join Hill on the Williamsburg Road. By this movement, the two converging columns became one very large force packed into a very narrow space so that it could only attack frontally and with a fraction of its force at a time.

MAJOR GENERAL
DANIEL H. HILL

(LC)

BATTERY A, 2ND U.S.
ARTILLERY AFTER
THE BATTLE OF
SEVEN PINES.

(LC)

The second factor complicating Johnston's attack was the weather. On the night of May 30, a raging storm lashed the Chickahominy basin. "Torrents of rain drenched the earth," recalled an awed General Keyes, "the thunder bolts rolled and fell without intermission, and the heavens flashed with a perpetual blaze of lightning." The deluge turned the river into a furious flood and swelled small tributaries beyond fordability. Slippery mud made the Confederates' task of moving large numbers of men over small roads even more difficult than it already was.

Finally, the imprecision of Johnston's instructions to his generals would contribute to the confusion. Huger suffered most from Johnston's muddled orders, and the mud and high water in creeks and streams coupled with Longstreet's crowding onto the Williamsburg Road delayed Huger's march by several hours.

The scheduled dawn attack did not begin until 1 P.M., when an impatient D. H. Hill sent his brigades forward unsupported.

Immediately in the path of Hill's men, hunkered down in flooded rifle pits, lay the novices of Silas Casey's division. Casey himself admitted that his men were ill trained and poorly equipped, and though the general was working diligently at making his men better soldiers, he knew they probably were not ready for a fight. D. H. Hill's men were about to accelerate the learning process for Casey's green Yankees. The Federal line shuddered under Hill's initial blow, some units broke and ran, but as the crucial minutes passed it became clear that Casey's untested rookies would hold their ground and fight. Still, the attacking Confederate force was too large for Casey to handle alone, so as his men withdrew deliberately he called for reinforcements. Casey's corps commander, Keyes, was slow in sending supports to threatened points, and Hill's men continued advancing.

The recent downpours had turned part of the battlefield into a swamp and flooded rifle pits and entrenchments. Confederate regiments went forward through hip-deep water, and officers had to form details to follow along behind the battle line and prop up the wounded against trees to prevent their drowning. The volume of fire was terrific, and men on both sides fell in incredible numbers. An Alabama colonel was so engrossed by the effort to save his regiment that he considered it his duty to ignore a personal tragedy. Colonel John B. Gordon passed his brother, a 19-year-old captain. "He had been shot through the lungs and was bleeding profusely," recalled Gordon. "I did not stop; I could not stop, nor would

he permit me to stop. There was no time for that—no time for anything except to move on and fire on."

About 4:40 P.M., D. H. Hill, strengthened by reinforcements from Longstreet, surged forward to hit a new Federal line near Seven Pines, this one anchored by troops under Brigadier General Samuel P. Heintzelman, commander of the Third Corps. Heintzelman's line held, even after a lone Confederate brigade commanded by Colonel Micah Jenkins stove in Heintzelman's right flank. Unsupported, Jenkins had to retire when the Federals brought up reserves.

Johnston remained near his headquarters through the early part of the day. He had not heard from Longstreet and did not know about the altered plan, but by mid-morning, he knew something had gone seriously wrong. About 4 P.M., Johnston received a note from Longstreet

asking his commander to join the battle. Puzzled and still in the dark, Johnston went forward with three brigades of Smith's Division (under W. H. C. Whiting). Near Fair Oaks Station on the railroad, Johnston's column encountered resistance. These Federals finally halted the Confederate column but only when reinforcements arrived after one of the more remarkable forced marches of the war.

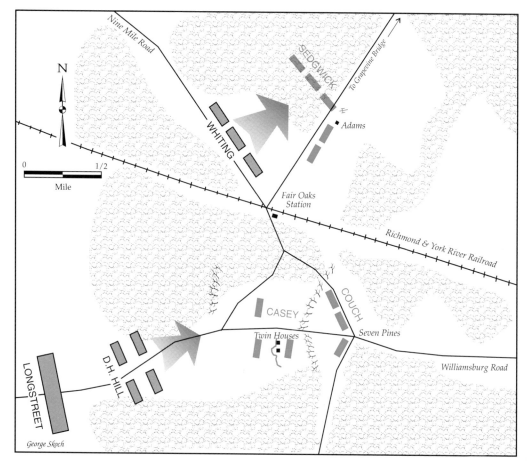

George Skoch

BATTLE OF SEVEN PINES—MAY 31 After a morning of confused and misunderstood orders, the Confederates finally struck McClellan's advance at Seven Pines. Silas Casey's untried division fell back to Seven Pines intersection, where reinforcements halted the Southern advance. Army commander Joseph E. Johnston fell wounded while watching his troops in action near Fair Oaks Station.

23

When Brigadier General Edwin V. Sumner, commander of the Second Corps on the north side of the Chickahominy, heard the sounds of battle at Seven Pines, he, on his own initiative, sent troops forward as reinforcements. His men had to cross the swift and turbulent waters of the rain-swollen river, but the only crossing available was Grapevine Bridge, which was partially submerged and threatening to wash away at any moment. Sumner ordered his men on to the groaning, swaying span. The weight of the passing column helped the bridge hold against the rushing waters, but soon after the last man reached the south bank, the timbers collapsed and were borne away by the roiling stream. Sumner's men, led by Brigadier General John Sedgwick, hastened forward and arrived on the battlefield in time to play a key part in halting Johnston's advance.

The most important event of the day —perhaps of the war—occurred near Fair Oaks Station late in the afternoon. Johnston, who had been actively exhorting his troops since entering the battle, suddenly reeled in his saddle, struck by a bullet and a piece of shrapnel. Anguished aides carried him to Richmond and out of the Peninsula campaign. With Johnston disabled, command of the army fell to G. W. Smith, who was bedeviled by ill health and, so it seemed, excessive caution. Davis felt he could not lay the fate of Richmond in such uncertain hands and that night made his most important decision of the war. Effective the next day, June 1, Robert E. Lee would command the army in the field.

Before Lee assumed command at Seven Pines on June 1, the armies at Seven Pines resumed the battle. The Confederates fended off Federal attacks

and ventured counterassaults that made no headway against fresh Federal troops in strong positions. The fighting ended leaving 6,100 Confederates and 5,000 Federals killed, wounded, captured, or missing in the two-day fight. It had been the bloodiest battle of the war in the East to that point, and only the armies engaged at the Battle of Shiloh in Tennessee on April 6 and 7 had killed or wounded more men than fell at Seven Pines (or Fair Oaks as the Federals called it).

Seven Pines marked the end of a phase in the Peninsula campaign. The large, climactic battle Johnston had wished and McClellan had expected had been attempted, but while Seven Pines had been large, it had not been climactic. McClellan called the battle a victory, but his army had been hurt and had very little to show for the win except that it had not been destroyed. Confederate leaders had much more reason to be depressed at the outcome of Seven Pines. Southerners had based their hopes of saving Richmond and their young nation on the premise that Confederate troops would at the moment of crisis somehow defeat the overwhelming invading hordes in battle —but when the battle came, the Yankees had survived. McClellan's army stood ready to resume its march on Richmond. After Seven Pines, the already darkening future of the Confederacy arguably took on a deeper hue of gloom.

On the morning of June 3, a pale, gaunt figure rode briskly through the forests above the Chickahominy. Erect in the saddle, well dressed, and with an air

of authority, he rode away from the city and toward the army. Jefferson Davis wished to see his troops, the men who would fight for him, the only ones now who could save his country.

Lee made a point of finding the president and joined him for an impromptu conference among the swamps. The two men had worked closely for months, but now the relationship was different. No longer would Lee simply offer suggestions or attend to administrative tasks. Now the

general was in command. He would direct the army, devise its strategies, and order its movements. The president and the general sat together that morning and talked. Having served for months as the president's military adviser, Lee now

The battles on the Peninsula wrought carnage that could scarcely be imagined by Americans of 1862. In just two months, more men were wounded on the fields east of Richmond than in all of America's previous wars combined. The two days of battle at Seven Pines produced as many injured men as the entire Revolutionary War, and more soldiers fell shot or torn in one afternoon at Gaines's Mill than did in the War of 1812 and the Mexican War put together.

Understandably, neither side was prepared for the unimaginable. Dr. Charles Tripler, medical director of the Army of the Potomac, was quickly overwhelmed and could find little room for battle casualties in hospitals already crammed with thousands of sick soldiers. Even worse was that Tripler had not enough ambulances, doctors, nurses, or medical supplies to deal with the crisis. The Federals averted a medical tragedy only through the selflessness of the scores of civilian volunteers who went to the Peninsula to ease the sufferings of the sick and wounded. Though many volunteers came forward on their own, the majority went to the Peninsula with the U.S. Sanitary Commission, a private organization founded by Northern benefactors and composed mainly of volunteer doctors, young women nurses, and medical students. One nurse stated that the commission's goal was to see "that every man had a good place to sleep in, and something hot to eat, and that the very sick had every essential that could have been given them in their own homes."

These volunteers freely criticized the army's handling of the wounded, especially after Seven Pines. "Conceive of the medical director," wrote a commission nurse at the White House Landing hospital, "sending down over 4,500 wounded without anything for them: without surgeons, with no one authorized to take charge of them, with nothing but empty boats to receive them. No stores, no beds, no hospital stewards, no food, no stimulants—there was nothing of the kind on any of the boats, and not a pail or a cup to distribute food, had there been any."

The commission set up a kitchen by the railroad tracks at White House, and to the sick and wounded arriving from the front the ladies doled out hot coffee with condensed milk and distributed brandy or wine or oranges or iced lemonade. Stretcher-bearers moved the soldiers onto commission hospital transports, which had been extensively fitted out at private expense. On these ships, the ill or injured would be moved to the more adequate care of hospitals in the North.

Confederate military medical personnel were no better prepared for the tide of bloody soldiers that flowed back from the battlefields. Chimborazo Hospital, the largest and perhaps the best hospital in Richmond at that time, had beds for 3,000 patients and a regular staff

asked the president to advise him. What should they do? How should they save Richmond? The question sprang from the very essence of Robert E. Lee. The Virginian already had strong opinions on what must be done to save the capital. He wanted to act on these plans, but he respected Davis, both personally and because the president was, by statute, commander in chief of the military. Lee also knew he needed the president's support, so he asked for advice, not merely

UNION WOUNDED FROM SEVEN PINES WERE BROUGHT TO THIS INCONSPICUOUS DWELLING, TURNED INTO A TEMPORARY FIELD HOSPITAL LIKE MOST OF THE FARMHOUSES IN THE AREA.

(USAMHI)

headed by Dr. James Brown McCaw. Dr. McCaw, a professor at Richmond's Medical College of Virginia, was energetic and innovative in turning Chimborazo into an excellent facility, but in the wake of the battles east of the city, he found himself pitifully short of staff, supplies, and space. Like their Northern counterparts, Southern civilians stepped forward to fill the breech.

Young Richmonder Constance Cary Harrison recalled that on the first day of fighting at Seven Pines, anxiety for the safety of Richmond

soon became an unaffordable luxury as residents began to prepare for the arrival of the wounded. "Night brought a lull in the cannonading," she wrote, "people lay down dressed upon beds, but not to sleep, while the weary soldiers slept upon their arms. Early next morning the whole town was on the street. Ambulances, litters, carts, every vehicle that the city could produce, went and came with a ghastly burden; those who could walk limped painfully home, in some cases so black with gunpowder they passed unrecog-

nized." Homes, churches, hotels, warehouses, and empty buildings throughout the city became hospitals and thousands of Richmonders, wealthy and impoverished alike, became angels of mercy. Men served as stretcher-bearers, ambulance drivers, or hospital stewards. Women who were not working as nurses gathered pew cushions from the city's churches and sewed them into beds for the wounded. "Larders all over town were emptied into baskets," recalled Harrison, and "the residents of those pretty houses standing back in gardens full of roses set their cooks to work, or, better still, went themselves into the kitchen, to compound delicious messes for the wounded."

More than 33,000 Northern and Southern soldiers suffered nonmortal wounds on the Peninsula, and army surgeons, volunteers, and citizens gamely tried to comfort the fallen and to save lives and limbs, but, as Miss Harrison noted after the ordeal ended, "all that was done was not enough by half."

to flatter his president, but as an assurance that he was willing to work as a team and that he valued the Mississippian's views.

Davis, equally as courteous and respectful, immediately responded by expressing his full confidence in Lee. They had already discussed Lee's outline of a plan—a swift movement to Richmond by Jackson's troops from the Valley, followed by a sudden move on the Federals' poorly positioned right flank. Davis told Lee he knew of no better plan than this and urged the general to enact it. The two men were of one mind: to defend Richmond, they must attack.

Lee at once went to work in refitting the army and preparing it again for battle. He ordered the earthen fortifications

around Richmond strengthened so they might be made secure by fewer troops, freeing more men for offensive operations. He consulted often with Davis and ordered troops from other parts of the Confederacy to move to Richmond in preparation for the offensive. What Lee hoped for most was that McClellan would not attack him before he could complete his preparations. Lee wished for time.

At the same time, McClellan repeatedly asked

Washington for reinforcements. His agents reported correctly that the Confederates were gathering strength in Richmond, though the spies overestimated the number of the massing Southerners. McClellan declared he needed more men to counter the Confederate buildup, and though the War Department had sent McClellan more than 30,000 additional men by mid-June, the general repeatedly asked for more.

Through the summer weeks on the Chickahominy, the Confederates spent their time digging and reorganizing, and many of the men, from officer to private, wondered about their new commander. Robert E. Lee was virtually unknown to the great majority of Americans. He had spent 37 of his 55 years laboring in obscurity in the U.S. Army as a military engineer, building levees and seacoast fortifications all across America, and as a commander of cavalry on the Texas frontier. His brother officers thought well of him, his superiors valued him, but to the rank and file he was a mystery. So far in the war, Lee had done little to suggest to the public that he was a great general, and with the Federals bearing down upon the capital and the Confederacy facing its greatest crisis, many questioned if Lee could rise to the hour. One of Joseph Johnston's former staff officers, Major E. P. Alexander, sat in conversation one day with Colonel Joseph C. Ives, of President Davis's staff. Ives knew Lee from the latter's months as adviser to the president, and Alexander, eager for Ives's insights on the new general, spoke frankly. "Has Gen. Lee the *audacity* that is going to be required for our inferior force to meet the enemy's superior force," he asked, "to take the aggressive, and to run risks and stand chances?" Ives answered without hesitation. "Alexander, if there is one man in either army, Confederate or Federal, head and shoulders above every other in *audacity*, it is Gen. Lee! His name might be audacity. He will take more desperate chances and take them quicker than any other general in this country, North or

South; and you will live to see it, too."

Though Lee's audacity remained to be seen, he daily revealed his thoroughness as a planner. He understood the strengths and weaknesses of the Federal position. He saw the railroad as an Achilles' heel, a tactical liability for McClellan, but Lee believed the Federal commander would cling to this necessary evil as long as possible. Furthermore, despite the critical importance of the rails to the Army of the Potomac, Lee suspected that McClellan's force north of the river was not properly placed to defend the railroad. The Virginian thought he might be able to maneuver a large force around McClellan's exposed flank north of Mechanicsville. If he succeeded in this and reached or seriously threatened the Federal supply line, Lee thought McClellan might abandon his supply line and flee—either southward to the protection of the U.S. Navy gunboats in the James River, or eastward, toward White House or Fort Monroe. In either case, Lee would have forced McClellan away from Richmond and, at the very least, bought the Confederacy more time.

Before he acted on this plan, however, Lee needed information. He called for his chief of cavalry, Brigadier General James Ewell Brown (Jeb) Stuart, and ordered the 29-year-old to explore the Federal right flank. Lee needed to know the exact position of the Federal line as well as its strength. Adventurous of spirit, Stuart wished to expand the reconnaissance into something more elaborate, something extraordinary, and determined to move deep into the Federal rear if the opportunity offered.

Stuart kept the assignment a secret until 2 A.M. on June 12, when he declared to his staff: "Gentlemen, in 10 minutes every man must be in his saddle." In the predawn darkness, Stuart led 1,200 picked troopers northward. Only Stuart knew where they were bound. The column moved an easy 22 miles that day, far to the north and west of the Federals' position near Mechanicsville, before Stuart ordered a halt. He wished his men to be well rested for tomorrow's work.

The next morning, June 13, the Southerners set off early and continued around the Federal flank. The Confederates ran into U.S. cavalry at

Hanover Court House and though the surprised and outnumbered Unionists fled, they spread the alarm, and more Federal cavalry converged to intercept the Southern column. At a crossroads called Linney's, Stuart encountered a strong line of Federal horsemen and at once ordered a charge. Captain William Latané of the 9th Virginia Cavalry, sabered Captain William Royall of the 5th U.S. Cavalry, but Royall won the encounter with two shots of his revolver. Latané fell dead, the first, and as it would turn out, only, Confederate fatality of Stuart's raid.

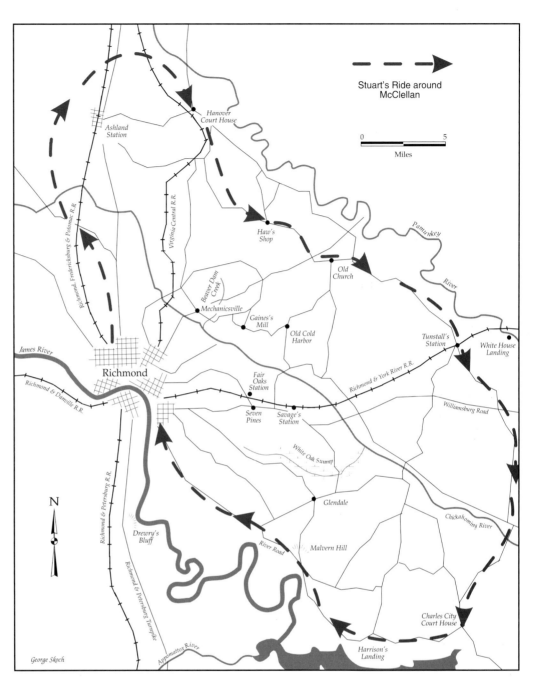

SEVEN DAYS'
BATTLES—
AREA MAP

*On June 12, 1862,
Brigadier General Jeb
Stuart led 1,200
troopers on one of the
more famous cavalry
rides of the war. Sent
by General Lee to
scout the Union right
flank near Mechan-
icsville, Stuart turned
the affair into a
three-day, 100-mile
ride that carried his
force completely
around McClellan's
army. Stuart's success
paid immediate divi-
dends. It provided Lee
with important intel-
ligence on the Union
position and acted
like an electric shock
to awaken a sagging
Southern morale.
Nevertheless, the ride
produced a fair
amount of controver-
sy. Critics suggested
that Stuart's action
helped alert
McClellan to the
dangers of his
position astride the
Chickahominy River,
thus hastening his
change of base from
the Pamunkey to the
James River.*

The raiders pushed deeper into the Federal rear, and by midday, Stuart had accomplished his mission; he knew where McClellan's flank was and had gained an idea of its strength. But the cavalryman was far from finished. He decided that the Federals, aware by now of his presence, would soon be after him in considerable numbers and might even now be closing upon his rear to seal off his escape route. He decided it might be as dangerous to retrace his steps as it would be to seek another route home. Stuart informed his officers that they would not turn back but ride on and pass completely around the Federal army before returning to Richmond.

The Federal pursuit, a part of which was managed by Stuart's father-in-law, Federal Brigadier General Philip St. George Cooke, was ineffective. The Southern horsemen rode all day and all night of the thirteenth, easily outdistancing their pursuers. Stuart's men took time

to damage the railroad at Tunstall's Station and burned 75 captured wagons and a schooner full of hay on the Pamunkey. By afternoon of June 14, Stuart and his sleepless men were across the Chickahominy and headed toward the James. The danger of Federal pursuit had long since passed so the weary column headed northwestward for Richmond at a more leisurely pace. The cavaliers soon arrived among friends, and the spectacular exploit soon made headlines, instantly transforming Stuart into one of the South's premier heroes.

Lee was pleased to learn that McClellan's flank was still vulnerable, and he at once put his attack plan into action. On June 16, the day after Stuart returned and reported his findings, Lee directed Stonewall Jackson to move his troops out of the Shenandoah Valley and toward Richmond in preparation for a movement on McClellan's right.

Lee knew that, even making use of the Virginia Central Railroad, Jackson would need several days to move his 18,500 men across Virginia and into position to attack, but the commander wished to have all the details of the attack ironed out before the troops arrived. Lee asked Jackson to meet with him, and the Valley

general headed for his commander's headquarters at the first opportunity. Lee summoned three other generals he would burden with responsibility in the coming battle to deliver Richmond. In the afternoon of June 23, Jackson, having ridden more than 50 miles ahead of his troops, arrived at the widow Mary Dabbs's house on the Nine Mile Road east of Richmond. Major General D. H. Hill, Jackson's brother-in-law, soon arrived, as did division commanders James Longstreet and Major General A. P. Hill, and the five men got down to business.

Lee informed his four generals that they were to attack McClellan within days and that the purpose of their meeting was to complete a plan and set a timetable. Jackson had the farthest to travel to get in position, so the timing of the attack

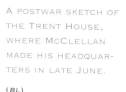

hinged upon his ability to move his column. After some discussion, the generals agreed that Jackson's arrival would begin the assault on the morning of June 26. The meeting closed, and Jackson remounted and rode more than 40 miles back to his command.

The next day, Lee issued Special Orders Number 75 specifying each general's role in the operation. According to the plan, Jackson's command was to camp south of Hanover Court House by the evening of June 25, ready to march at 3 A.M. on the twenty-sixth, thus triggering the attack. He was to stay well north of the Federal position at Mechanicsville and move toward Cold Harbor. After Jackson moved, Lawrence O'B. Branch's brigade, of A.P. Hill's division, was to cross the Chickahominy at Half Sink, fall in on the Valley general's right flank, and advance toward Mechanicsville. A. P. Hill, waiting on the Meadow Bridges Road south of the Chickahominy, was to cross as soon as he discovered the movements of Jackson and Branch and move directly upon Mechanicsville. After Hill drove the Union forces through Mechanicsville (the Federals, Lee hoped, would be eager to abandon their strong positions at Beaver

A. P. HILL'S MEN PASSED THROUGH THE HAMLET OF MECHANICSVILLE BEFORE STRIKING THE MAIN FEDERAL LINE ALONG BEAVER DAM CREEK.

(USAMHI)

Dam Creek because Jackson would have by then outflanked them), the way would be open for Longstreet and D. H. Hill to cross the Chickahominy on the Mechanicsville Turnpike. Once that was accomplished, Lee would have consolidated 60,000 troops on the north bank of the Chickahominy. Together, the four columns would then, in Lee's words, "sweep down the Chickahominy, and endeavor to drive the enemy from his positions. . . . Then press forward towards the York River Railroad, closing upon the enemy's rear and forcing him down the Chickahominy." This was the hand the gambler Lee was about to play, and, as Major E. P. Alexander later wrote, "the stakes were already his if his execution were even half as good as his plan."

McClellan had spent much of June 23 and 24 thinking about attacks as well. A stretch of dry weather had helped solidify the roads, and recent reinforcements had brought the army's strength to 115,000. The general declared it was almost time to act. He desired the high ground at a crossroads known as Old Tavern on the Nine Mile Road above Fair Oaks Station. From this vantage point, he expected to be able to dominate enough of the surrounding country to emplace heavy artillery that would force the Confederates from their advanced fortifications. By repeating this process of "regular advances," McClellan hoped to move step by step to within perhaps a couple of miles of Richmond, where his heavy artillery could bombard the Confederate capital. "Then," he wrote, "I shall shell the city and take it by assault." He planned to capture Old Tavern on the twenty-sixth or twenty-seventh and scheduled a preliminary assault south of the crossroads for

June 25. It was, he said, the first step toward taking Richmond.

On the rainy morning of June 25, Third Corps commander Sam Heintzelman sent Joe Hooker's division forward with orders to capture a thick patch of woods in no-man's-land between the Federal and Confederate lines. McClellan desired control of the woods so he would know what the Confederates were up to on the far side. Troops from both the Second and Fourth Corps would do some fighting this day, but Hooker's men would bear the brunt of the combat in what they would come to call the Battle of Oak Grove.

Opposing Hooker on the far side of the woods were the men of Brigadier General Ambrose R. Wright's brigade. Wright's 4th Georgia was on picket that morning and opened the battle with men of the 1st and 11th Massachusetts. For most of the day, the fight would tear through the woods and fields before the Confederate works. The troops engaged had had little or no experience in combat, and the battle was an ugly, clumsily managed affair. By 5 P.M., McClellan, who had watched part of the battle in the afternoon, declared to the War Department that he had won the battle and with little loss. He was premature on both counts, however, for about a half hour later, Wright launched a counterattack that did little damage to the Federal position but piled up more casualties. By the time the firing stopped well after dark, Wright, like McClellan,

claimed victory, but considering that together the armies had lost more than 1,100 men and that the position of the front lines had changed little, history would declare the Battle of Oak Grove (or King's Schoolhouse, as the Confederates called it) a costly and indecisive draw. Neither side knew that Oak Grove was merely the first fight in a week of unimagined bloodshed that would become known as the Seven Days' Battle.

Toward sunset on the twenty-fifth, the rain began to peter out, and anxious citizens in Richmond looking eastward toward the battlefield saw what many thought was an omen. A rainbow stood out against the darkening sky. None of the people knew it, but with the conclusion of the fighting at Oak Grove, McClellan's offensive operations against Richmond ceased. The Confederates had withstood the worst McClellan would give them, and the morning of June 26 would mark the dawn of a new era in Confederate history.

Lee fretted for a while on the night of the twenty-fifth that McClellan's advance at Oak Grove had been a spoiling attack. On the morning of the twenty-sixth, Lee wrote to Davis: "I fear from the operations of the enemy yesterday that our plan of operations has been discov-

ered to them." But by the time he turned in on the night of the twenty-fifth, Lee had already made his decision to proceed with his plan—it would not be ruined by McClellan's foray. Lee went to bed believing that the situation was well in hand and tomorrow would see the first step in the deliverance of Richmond.

June 26 dawned pleasant, but as Lee prepared to move to the battlefield, he received displeasing news: Jackson sent word that he was far behind schedule. He said he would have his command up and on the road earlier than planned, but Lee knew Jackson would be unable to be at his assigned place on time. The commanding general could only hope Jackson would move as rapidly as possible and make up much of the lost time. Lee joined Longstreet's column on the dusty Mechanicsville Turnpike to wait and from bluffs above the Chickahominy watched Federal pickets in and around the hamlet of Mechanicsville on the other side of the river. The generals listened for the sounds of firing from A. P. Hill's front two miles upstream signaling the arrival of Jackson, but the air hung heavy, hot, and silent.

Around 10 A.M., Lawrence Branch, waiting farther upstream from Hill's position, received a note from Jackson and learned that the Valley army was still behind schedule but was at last crossing the Virginia Central Railroad into the day's area of operations. Jackson had not begun his day's march as early as he had hoped to and once on the road had encountered fallen trees, enemy skirmishers, and other obstacles thrown in his path by Fitz John Porter's men. The result was that only by late morning on the twenty-sixth was Jackson reaching the place he was to have camped on the night of the twenty-fifth. By the most generous estimate, Jackson was more than four hours—about 12 miles—behind where he should have been.

Having at last heard from Jackson, Branch crossed the Chickahominy and headed for Mechanicsville in execution of his part of the plan, but his brigade of North Carolinians would not get into the fight that day, nor would Jackson's 18,500 Valley troops. The man who initiated the battle on June 26 had tired of waiting for Jackson and Branch and, in his own words, "determined to cross [the Chickahominy] at once rather than hazard the failure of the whole plan by longer deferring it." Thirty-six-year-old A. P. Hill, youngest of Lee's division commanders, was restless by nature, and by 3 P.M. he was out of patience. Having heard from neither Jackson nor Branch, he ordered his men to force a crossing at Meadow Bridges. The vastly outnumbered Federal pickets gave

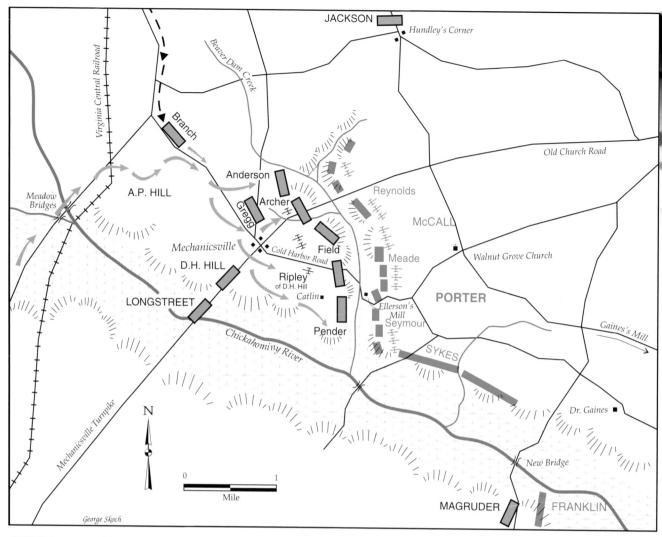

SEVEN DAYS' BATTLES: DAY TWO—JUNE 26, BATTLE OF BEAVER DAM CREEK

After waiting in vain for word from Stonewall Jackson, Brigadier General A. P. Hill put Lee's battle plan into motion by crossing the Chickahominy River at Meadow Bridges. Skirmishing quickly developed as Hill's brigades drove through Mechanicsville. Meanwhile, Brigadier General George McCall's division of Pennsylvania Reserves occupied previosly built fortifications behind Beaver Dam Creek. Despite repeated attempts, Union infantry and artillery repulsed each effort to break their lines. That evening McClellan ordered a withdrawal. The next day Brigadier General Fitz John Porter and the V Corps held an equally strong position behind Boatswain's Creek.

way, and Hill pushed on to Mechanicsville.

Lee, watching from the bluffs above the Chickahominy, saw Confederate troops enter the village and exclaimed "Those are A. P. Hill's men." Lee had intended that there be no real fighting at Mechanicsville. Jackson's force should have outflanked the Federals at Mechanicsville by late morning or early afternoon, and the Northerners should have withdrawn of their own volition, but here was Hill forcing his way through against stronger-than-expected resistance.

Lee rode forward to learn what had gone wrong with the plan.

Hill still expected Jackson to make an appearance above the headwaters of Beaver Dam Creek, so he focused his attacks on the Federal right flank. He sent Brigadier General Joseph R. Anderson's brigade to assault the Federals north of Mechanicsville above the Old Church Road, closest to where he expected Jackson to arrive.

Beaver Dam Creek, a tributary of the Chickahominy, flowed almost due south

less than a mile east of Mechanicsville. The Federals had recognized the great natural strength of the position and built a line of rifle pits and artillery emplacements on the bluffs above the eastern bank of the stream. When Hill's men advanced through Mechanicsville, the defenses of Beaver Dam Creek were manned by the Pennsylvania Reserves Division, some 8,000 men under the command of Brigadier General George A. McCall. McCall's men were recent arrivals

to the Peninsula and had gone into position at Beaver Dam Creek just days before Lee launched his attack.

As Hill's men deployed in lines of battle and went forward, McCall's artillery opened, dividing its attention between the infantry and a few Confederate batteries, which were soon silenced with heavy loss. As the Southern infantry moved down the slope into the stream bottom, McCall's infantry, ensconced in their rifle pits, prepared for action. A Pennsylvania private remembered his major encouraging him and his comrades to "give them hell, or get it ourselves." Hill's men pressed ever closer, but the Northerners waited. "We did not fire a shot until they came up within 100 yards of us," wrote Federal private Enos Bloom. "Then we gave them what the Major told us to give them." Brigadier General John F. Reynolds rode along his battle line pointing out targets to his Pennsylvanians: "Look at them, boys, in the swamp there, they are as thick as flies on a ginger bread; fire low, fire low." Another of McCall's privates recalled that "the enemy charged bayonets on us three times, but we cut them down . . . I fired until my gun got so hot that I could barely hold it in my hands." "We piled them up by the hundreds," reported Private Bloom, "making a perfect bridge across the swamp."

Despite such withering fire, enough Confederates made it across the creek to give the Second Pennsylvania Reserves some anxious moments. "At one time they charged the left and the centre at the same time," recalled one officer, "boldly pressing on their flags until they nearly met ours, when the fighting became of the most desperate character, the flags rising and falling as they were surged to and fro by the contending parties. . . . Our left was driven back, the enemy . . . bending our line into a convexed circle." These were the men of the 35th Georgia, whom Anderson had sent toward the extreme Federal flank in the hope of flanking the Pennsylvanians, but the Georgians failed and were thrown back with heavy loss.

To the south, Hill pushed more brigades into action at Ellerson's Mill. To reach the stream, the Confederates had to cross a broad plateau while Federal artillery across the creek hammered away at them. A Virginia battery boldly came forward and was smashed, losing 42 of 92 men and many horses. Brigadier General Dorsey Pender's brigade strode toward the mill and felt the sting of more than a dozen Federal cannon and supporting infantry. Pender's assault, like those before it, failed to dent the Federal line. After 6 P.M., Lee found Brigadier General Roswell Ripley's Brigade in Mechanicsville and, believing the Federals were vulnerable near Ellerson's Mill, ordered Ripley to attack. The slaughter was horrible as the Pennsylvanians, secure behind their breastworks, loaded and fired at the open targets as rapidly as they could. Ripley's

men fell as hay before a scythe. His 44th Georgia alone lost 324 men—60 percent of the regiment's strength.

Darkness closed upon the scene of suffering, ending the combat and initiating a night of torment for the hundreds of wounded men lying in the swamp. This first battle of Lee's career with the Army of Northern Virginia was a stinging defeat, costing him 1,500 men, about 10 percent of his force engaged, in exchange for fewer than 400 Federals.

Despite the setbacks, delays, and bloody sacrifices of the day, Lee's plan was working, albeit too slowly and not exactly as had been intended. Jackson had reached his assigned place at Pole Green Church late in the day. He was then on the Federal flank above the headwaters of Beaver Dam Creek, just where Lee wished him to be. Although Hill was at the same moment making no progress in forcing the Federals from their works, the Northerners' position was, thanks to Jackson, already untenable, though Fitz John Porter did not yet know it.

The Federals could not long remain at Beaver Dam Creek with Jackson on their flank, and as soon as McClellan

SOME OF THE HOTTEST FIGHTING AT BEAVER DAM CREEK CENTERED AROUND ELLERSON'S MILL WHERE MASSED FEDERAL ARTILLERY AND ENTRENCHED UNION INFANTRY REPULSED REPEATED CONFEDERATE CHARGES.

(NA)

confirmed Jackson's presence that night, he ordered Porter to withdraw. McCall's men were angry that they had to abandon the positions they had successfully defended and even angrier that McClellan's order came to them just before dawn and they had to leave so hastily that they could not prepare an adequate rear guard. The Confederates advanced promptly in the morning and captured scores of McCall's men attempting to cover the retreat of Porter's corps.

That Thursday morning, June 27, must have found Robert E. Lee pleased with the progress of events. His plan,

though still behind schedule, was unfolding satisfactorily, and both his army and part of McClellan's were moving in the direction he wished—down the Chickahominy. But Lee was far from being content and knew that his troops must keep the pressure on Porter's men if the Federals were to be forced from the north bank of the Chickahominy. Again this day Jackson's command would play the crucial part in the plan. He was to continue his march to Old Cold Harbor, still moving along the Federal right flank. As Lee saw it, the Federals, aware now of Jackson's presence, had two choices: they could prepare to meet Jackson when he arrived on their flank and rear at Old Cold Harbor or they could abandon altogether their positions north of the Chickahominy. Lee hoped it would be the latter. He met with Jackson at Walnut Grove Church and, as the army's columns pressed by in dusty pursuit, informed his general that D. H. Hill's large division would march with the Valley army and be under Jackson's command. The two men parted, Jackson to move his men onward

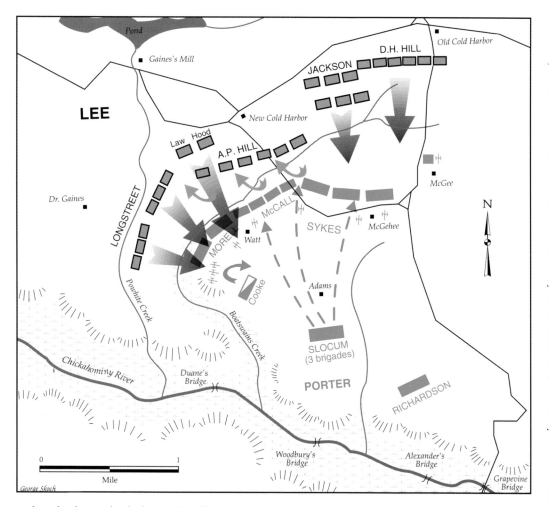

Map labels:
Pond
Gaines's Mill
Old Cold Harbor
D.H. HILL
JACKSON
LEE
New Cold Harbor
Law Hood
A.P. HILL
McGee
Dr. Gaines
LONGSTREET
McCALL
MORE
Watt
SYKES
McGehee
N
Pouhite Creek
Cooke
Adams
Boatswains Creek
Chickahominy River
Duane's Bridge
SLOCUM
(3 brigades)
PORTER
RICHARDSON
0   1
Mile
George Skoch
Woodbury's Bridge
Alexander's Bridge
Grapevine Bridge

—they had marched about 10 miles already that morning and would have to cover another eight to be in position at Old Cold Harbor—and Lee to join A. P. Hill's and Longstreet's columns pursuing in the Federals' wake toward Gaines's Mill. If all went well, Lee would have all 60,000 men of his attacking force in position to fight by early afternoon.

But Fitz John Porter, a brave and capable officer, did not rattle easily. He and his friend McClellan had spent the night of June 26 discussing the situation of the army, and Porter understood that he was to be entrusted with fulfilling a crucial assignment. McClellan had decided the time had come to let go of his supply line—the Richmond & York River Railroad —and move toward the James to establish a new base. This would be a dangerous

operation in the presence of a large and aggressive enemy, but faced with the choice of standing and fighting or chang- ing his base, McClellan decided the retro- grade movement was the better

option. He needed time to move the army, its 3,000 wagons, heavy guns of the artillery reserve, the sick and wounded, the 2,500 head of beef, and countless tons of supplies, and Porter and his men would buy that time. If they failed, the army might be destroyed.

Reinforced to a strength of 35,000 men, Porter formed his defense on high ground east of Gaines's Mill and behind Boatswain's Creek. Like the line at Beaver Dam Creek, this naturally strong position rose to wooded heights that dominated a boggy creek bottom, but Porter's men made it even stronger by felling trees and digging rifle pits on the steep slope and placing batteries along the top of the hill. For the second consecutive day, the Federals had a great advantage in a dominating defensive position.

A. P. Hill's men began the action around 2:30 P.M., testing Porter's position near New Cold Harbor. Hill later reported that "the incessant roar of musketry and the deep thunder of the artillery" told him that the Federals were before him in great strength. His men, the general wrote, "met a withering storm of bullets, but pressed on to within a short distance of the enemy's works, but the storm was too fierce . . . they recoiled and were again pressed to a charge, but with no better success. These brave men had done all that any soldiers could do." The Federals repulsed all Confederate sallies throughout the afternoon, and hundreds of men, Union and Confederate, fell on the slopes above the creek bottom.

Daylight waned, and Lee had yet to crack the Federal line. Though A. P. Hill and Longstreet had been feeding men into the fight all afternoon, they had made no substantial progress. Much to the commanding general's frustration, Longstreet and Hill lacked support from the left end of the Confederate line. For the second time in two days, Stonewall Jackson was late.

Lacking good maps and led by a guide who misunderstood his instructions, Jackson had taken a wrong road and lost precious time. Only late in the afternoon did his men reach Old Cold Harbor and deploy for battle. At 7 P.M., Lee ordered a general assault, and soon thereafter, Confederate infantry advanced along a two-mile front. The persistent Southerners pressed in on the outnumbered Federals at every point along the line. The firing was terrific, producing a defeaning roar and clouds of smoke that one Texan swore blocked out the sun.

Finally, as the sun was setting, portions of Porter's line began to give way. Brigadier General John Hood's "Texas Brigade" broke through at Boatswain's Creek, and, on the far eastern end of the line, Jackson's men breached the Federal defense near the road to the Chickahominy. Despite heroic resistance in some places, especially by the U.S. Regular troops opposing Jackson, Porter's

ONE FAMILY'S WAR

Among the hundreds of civilians to feel the effects of invasion and war on the Peninsula the family of Hugh Watt stands out. Mr. Watt and his wife, Sarah, had operated a prosperous farm on the north bank of the Chickahominy River. Their modest plantation home Springfield was built in the early 1800s.

In the early afternoon of June 27, 1862, the Battle of Gaines's Mill erupted on the Watt Farm. The 77-year-old Mrs. Watt (by that time a widow) had been very ill for several weeks. As the first shells crashed into the stable and kitchen chimney, Union officers warned the family to leave quickly. Mrs. Watt protested feebly, but her children hastily moved her off to safety. One of her grandchildren recorded later that Mrs. Watt's condition had "benumbed her faculties," thus softening the anguish of departing the family farm. The largest battle in the history of Virginia up to that point was about to explode on her farm.

The Watts joined a procession of at least forty other displaced locals fleeing eastward beyond the borders of the battlefield. Occasionally some badly aimed shell would explode nearby, adding to the chaos. The refugees gathered together in small groups and listened to the battle "with bowed heads and tearful eyes."

At twilight, the final Confederate surge of the battle swept through the yard of the Watt House and beyond, leaving a trail of dead and wounded soldiers mixed with shattered wood from the house and its outbuildings. Victorious Confederates soon began to segregate the wounded, removing the injured Northerners they found into and around the house. One week later a Confederate surgeon reported 400 wounded still at the house. Supplies had dwindled, leaving the miserable collection of wounded "entirely unprovided for."

A visitor to the area in September noticed graves all over the yard, even in Mrs. Watt's garden. The house stood grimly silent, "The walls and roof . . . torn by shot and shell, the weatherboarding honeycombed by minnie balls, and every pane of glass shattered." Every piece of floor inside the house bore menacing bloodstains. "Once a neat and comfortable home now a . . . foul and battered wreck," the visitor concluded.

Mrs. Watt was spared the ugliness of the scene. Her condition continued to deteriorate, and she died early the following year, apparently without having returned home. In some ways Sarah Watt is similar to the famous Widow Henry at the Battle of First Manassas. Although Mrs. Henry died in more violent circumstances, they both illustrate the arbitrary heavy hand of the Civil War that doled out destruction to soldier and civilian alike.

SARAH BOHANNON KIDD WATT

(COURTESY OF ELIZABETH DEANE HAW HOBBS)

line began to crumble. In desperation, cavalry commander Philip St. George Cooke ordered a cavalry charge intended to throw the advancing Confederates off balance long enough for Federal infantry and artillery to escape. Cooke's charge failed, and the Federals lost 22 cannon and thousands of prisoners in the withdrawal.

The Battle of Gaines's Mill was a clear Confederate victory. Porter's force, outnumbered for much of the day, had held its own but at a fearful cost—about 6,000 Northerners killed, wounded, missing, or captured in seven hours of fighting. Lee had won his first battlefield victory at the steep price of 9,000 men. With almost 95,000 men engaged, Gaines's Mill was larger and costlier than Seven Pines and established a new standard for bloodletting in the eastern theater. Though the two armies that had battled at Shiloh several weeks before had produced almost

STONEWALL JACKSON'S TROOPS MARCHED PAST OLD COLD HARBOR TAVERN ON THEIR WAY TO BATTLE ON JUNE 27.

(BL)

25,000 casualties in two days of fighting, Lee and Porter had together lost 15,000 in a single afternoon.

McClellan saw the battle for the disaster it was, and he was ready to point the finger of blame. Throughout the campaign, the general had been pleading with Washington to send him reinforcements. He had reported (incorrectly) that the Confederates outnumbered him overwhelmingly and that his army was in great danger if not strengthened. Now, the doom he had foretold had become reality, and he was quick to blame it on Lincoln and the War Department.

"I have lost this battle because my force was too small," he wrote in a midnight letter just hours after the firing stopped. "I again repeat that I am not responsible for this, and say it with the earnestness of a general who feels in his heart the loss of every brave man who has needlessly been sacrificed to-day. . . .

You must send me very large reinforcements, and send them at once. . . . As it is, the government must not and cannot hold me responsible for the result."

The general then got to the heart of the matter. He felt his political enemies in Washington, among whom he numbered Secretary of War Edwin M. Stanton, had conspired to bring about his failure. "I feel too earnestly to-night," the general wrote, "I have seen too many dead and wounded comrades to feel otherwise that

the government has not sustained this army. If you do not do so now the game is lost. If I save this army now, I tell you plainly that I owe no thanks to you or to any other persons in Washington. You have done your best to sacrifice this army." A startled communications officer in Washington deleted the final two sentences before delivering the telegram to Stanton.

If McClellan's intemperate and insubordinate "I-told-you-so" letter was intended to send chills of fear through Lincoln and Stanton, it worked. Lincoln immediately responded with a kind, supportive note, assuring the general that the government would do everything possible to forward reinforcements, but that McClellan must do his best in the meantime to save the army.

McClellan was justified in his complaints to the extent that Washington had not been patient during the three months he had been on the Peninsula and had repeatedly badgered him to move more quickly on Richmond. From the Lincoln administration's point of view, however,

the campaign was an enormous drain on the Federal treasury, and Lincoln, Stanton, and their military advisers seem to have lost confidence in McClellan as the weeks dragged on. There seemed to be no end in sight. Furthermore, though the Lincoln administration had withheld troops from McClellan, they had also reinforced him

by almost 40,000 men between April and mid-June.

McClellan's plan for saving his army was complex. First, the supply officers had to relocate the enormous depot from White House Landing on the Pamunkey to an as-yet-undetermined point on the James River. Federal engineers searched for a site for the new depot even as the quartermasters packed up the old one. McClellan intended for his army to move rapidly from the Chickahominy over some 14 circuitous miles of narrow, country roads through dense forests to the James. He sent the Fourth Corps ahead to secure important points, especially the bridge over White Oak Swamp and the crucial crossroads of Glendale, through which most of the army must pass. Fitz John Porter's battered Fifth Corps would follow the Fourth Corps and move on to the

ONCE MCCLELLAN'S RETREAT BEGAN, NEARLY EVERY ROAD BETWEEN THE CHICKAHOMINY AND JAMES RIVERS WAS CLOGGED WITH MOVING MEN AND WAGONS.

(LC)

THE CONFEDERATE PERSPECTIVE AT GAINES'S MILL

The Battle of Gaines's Mill was the largest of the Seven Days' battles. The following graphic account, excerpted from a letter written by an unidentified member of the 4th Texas Infantry, captures one man's battlefield experience. It was published the month after the battle in one of the Richmond newspapers.

"Suddenly, we (4th Texas Regiment) faced to the front, advanced in a run up the hill, and as we reached the brow, were welcomed with a storm of grape and canister from the opposite hill side, while the two lines of infantry, protected by their works, and posted on the side of the hill, upon the top of which was placed their battery, poured deadly and staggering volleys full in our faces. Here fell our Colonel, John Marshall, and with him, nearly half of his regiment. On the brow of this hill the dead bodies of our Confederate soldiers lay in numbers. They who had gone in at this point before us, and had been repulsed, stopped on this hill to fire, and were mowed down like grass and compelled to retire. It was now past 5 o'clock. When we got to the brow of this hill,

instead of halting, we rushed down it, yelling, and madly plunged right into the deep branch of water at the base of the hill. Dashing up the steep bank, being within thirty yards of the enemy's works, we flew towards the breastworks, cleared them, and slaughtered the retreating devils as they scampered up the hill towards their battery. There a brave fellow, on horseback, with his hat on his sword, tried to rally them . . . leaping over the work, we dashed up the hill, driving them before us and capturing the battery.

. . . . we saw there was yet work ahead. We were now in an open field . . . a heavy thirty-two pound battery straight ahead now opened on us with terrible effect, while another off to the right reminded us that we had just commenced the battle. On we go . . . exposed to a galling fire from the battery in front, from that on the right, and from swarms of broken infantry all on our left and rear. Yet on, on we go, with not a field officer to lead us, two thirds of the Company officers and half the men already down—yelling, shouting, firing, running

straight up to the death-dealing machines before us; every one resolved to capture them and rout the enemy . . . I could plainly see the gunners at work; down they would drive the horrid grape—a long, blazing flame issued from the pieces, and then crashing through the fence and barn, shattering rails and weatherboarding, came the terrible missiles with merciless fury . . . The smoke had now settled down upon the field in thick curtains, rolling about like some half solid substance; the dust was suffocating. We could see nothing but the red blaze of the cannon, and hear nothing but its roar and the hurtling and whizzing of the missiles. Suddenly the word is passed down the line, "Cavalry," and down come horses and riders with sabres swung over their heads, charging like an avalanche upon our scattered lines; they were met by volleys of lead, and fixed bayonets in the hands of resolute men, and in less time that I take to write it, a squadron of U.S. Regular Cavalry was routed and destroyed. Horses without riders, or sometimes with a wounded or dead master dangling from the stirrups, plunged wildly and fearfully over the plain, trampling over dead and dying, presenting altogether one of the most sublime and at the same time fearful pictures that any man can conceive of without being an eyewitness . . . .

The next morning we arose early. I will not attempt to describe the appearance of the field. I could write twenty pages and yet give you no adequate idea of it."

Richmond Daily Whig
August 4, 1862

James. Meanwhile, the three other corps that had remained south of the river—the Second, Third, and Sixth, about 42,000 men total—would hold their positions around Seven Pines and Savage's Station and cover the retreat (McClellan declined to call the movement a retreat. Instead, he cast the sidling march to the James in a positive light and referred to it as a "change of base," as though it were merely another component of his offensive operations against Richmond). McClellan calculated that he would need two days —all of June 28 and 29—to get the lead two corps and all of his impedimenta (wagons, wounded, cattle, and so on) across White Oak Swamp, which he hoped would offer some measure of protection.

So far, Lee had been completely successful in his goal of driving McClellan from Richmond. Not only had he delivered the capital from the imminent threat of the siege, but he had wrested the initiative from McClellan. Lee was now deciding the course of events, and McClellan, on the defensive, was reacting to the Confederate's moves. Lee had reversed the pattern of the past three months in just two days.

But the Confederate commander was not satisfied to rest upon these accomplishments. He saw that now an even greater opportunity for success lay before him. The defeated and battered enemy was in flight—a circumstance every aggressive fighter hopes for, and Lee was no exception. He believed that if he pursued McClellan and could again strike him a hard blow, he might stand a very good chance of destroying the Federal army, or at least a large portion of it. Lee did not intend to permit McClellan to escape.

But first, Lee had to be sure of where McClellan was retreating to. The Federals might go to the James or they might move eastward toward White House or even Fort Monroe. The Virginian spent anxious hours on June 28 waiting for word from his scouts, but late in the day came evidence to convince him that McClellan was heading southward. Lee at once began planning to intercept and attack the Army of the Potomac somewhere between the Chickahominy and the James.

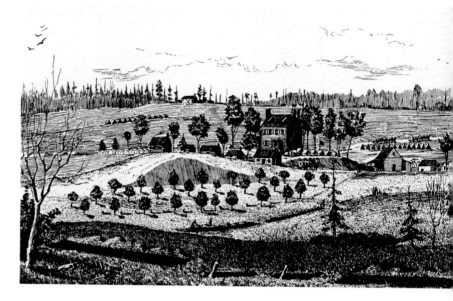

SAVAGE'S STATION ON
THE RICHMOND AND
YORK RIVER RAILROAD.

(BL)

According to Lee's new plan, Magruder, who had been holding the Confederate line south of the Chickahominy with 23,000 men against McClellan's approximately 58,000, was to move aggressively along the Williamsburg Road–York River Railroad corridor toward Savage's Station. Benjamin Huger, with his 9,000 men, was to move along Magruder's right flank on the Charles City Road and push toward what Lee saw was the crucial intersection at Glendale. Longstreet and A. P. Hill with 20,000 men total, were to make a long march westward toward Richmond then southward and eastward on the Darbytown Road heading, like Huger, for Glendale. Jackson's column,

including D. H. Hill's command, was to cross the Chickahominy and follow directly in McClellan's wake.

Savage's Station had been a Federal supply depot since just before the Battle of Seven Pines. McClellan's quartermasters had accumulated enormous amounts of food and equipment at the depot, and now, as the army began its retreat, the supply officers realized they could not remove everything. On June 28, the work of destruction began. Pennsylvania chaplain J. J. Marks wrote, "No language can paint the spectacle. Hundreds of barrels of flour and rice, sugar and molasses, salt and coffee, were consigned to the flames; and great heaps of these precious articles in a few moments lay scorching and smoldering. A long line of boxes of crackers, fifteen feet high, were likewise thrown into the mass."

While the destruction continued, a far sadder story began to unfold. Savage's Station also served as a Federal field hospital. After the battles of June 26 and 27, some 1,500 wounded men flooded into the hospital at Savage's, and more continued to arrive until more than 2,500 men lay in and around the tents at the depot. The surgeons were overwhelmed, as, apparently, was General McClellan. Though he had just hours earlier told the president in lavish rhetoric that he "feels in his heart the loss of every brave man who has needlessly been sacrificed," McClellan decided he could not evacuate the wounded and would abandon them to the mercy of the enemy.

Once again in this long campaign on the Peninsula, "Prince John" Magruder found himself in the limelight. Three months had passed since the Virginian had duped the Federals with theatrics at Yorktown. Now he was at the heart of Lee's plan to crush McClellan's army. Unfortunately, he was barely up to the task. Magruder had been ill and was taking medication laced with opium. He could not relax enough to sleep and seemed to some around him to be nearing the end of his endurance. Nevertheless the decisive hour was at hand, and Lee expected Magruder to do his duty. The general's orders were plain: press vigorously toward Savage's Station.

Magruder moved forward with 13,000 men on Sunday morning, June 29 and skirmished with Federals along the railroad. The Northerners, under General Sumner, made a stand near a peach orchard at Allen's Farm on the railroad but withdrew after delaying Magruder a couple of hours. The Confederates pushed on, but as they neared Savage's, Magruder began to grow apprehensive. Federal activity in his front convinced him he was about to be attacked, and he asked Lee for reinforcements. Lee likely discounted Magruder's fears but supported him with two extra brigades anyway, stipulating that the brigades must be returned if not used promptly. The Federal attack never came, and the two brigades trudged wearily back to where they belonged.

Lee had hoped to squeeze the Federal position at Savage's with pressure from Magruder on the west and Jackson on the north, but the latter was again mysteriously slow in fulfilling his assignment. His men worked to rebuild bridges over the Chickahominy, but the task took much longer than expected, and Jackson seems not to have pressed his men to get the job done with all haste. In the afternoon, Jackson received a copy of a note from headquarters that he believed ordered him to hold his position at the bridges. When an officer from Magruder's command asked Jackson why he was not

crossing the Chickahominy to attack Savage's Station, Jackson replied that he had "other important duties to perform." This puzzled both Magruder and Lee. The commanding general said Jackson had made a mistake and should be advancing vigorously. But the misunderstanding had gone too far to be reclaimed. Magruder was on his own and advanced cautiously.

After Sumner had withdrawn his Second Corps troops from Allen's Farm, he joined most of the Sixth Corps and Third Corps around Savage's. McClellan had moved on toward the James with the rest of the army without appointing anyone to command the rear guard, nor had

he issued any orders about deployment at Savage's. Sumner, the senior general present, did not quickly grasp the developing tactical situation and made no cohesive defensive deployment, but he would have little trouble fending off Magruder's tentative thrusts at Savage's Station. The Confederate sent only a few of his brigades forward into the woods and fields west of the station, and Sumner would send only a few in response. The Confederates, especially the brigades of Brigadier General Joseph B. Kershaw and

Brigadier General Paul J. Semmes, pressed on gallantly, inflicting severe punishment and threatening to breach the Federal line. Brigadier General William Burns's Philadelphians surged forward to stem the tide, and reinforcements from the large Federal reserve stifled all further Southern advances. When Brigadier General William T. H. Brooks's Vermont brigade stormed into the woods toward dusk, it ran smack into Semmes's men and Colonel William Barksdale's Mississippians. For a short time, the fight in the darkening woods matched anything Shiloh or Seven Pines or Gaines's Mill could boast in the way of ferocity. "In less time than it takes to tell it," recalled one of Brooks's men, "the ground was strewn with fallen Vermonters." The 5th Vermont lost 206 men, more than half its strength, in 20 minutes. Among the fallen were five Cummings brothers, one of their cousins, and their brother-in-law. Six of the seven men were killed; only the eldest brother, Henry Cummings, survived.

When the fighting stopped west of Savage's, almost 450 of Magruder's men had become casualties. The South Carolinians of Kershaw's Brigade got the worst of the fight, losing 290 men, and in a vain cause, for Magruder had not accomplished his mission or attained any significant strategic advantages. Later that night, Lee uncharacteristically expressed his dissatisfaction with Magruder's lack of progress. The commanding general saw that his opportunities to seriously harm the Federals were slipping away and told Magruder "we must waste no more time or he will escape us entirely."

That night held no rest for the Army of the Potomac. The men stumbled onward though the black forests and endured the lashings of a violent thunderstorm before dawn on June 30 found most of them south of White Oak Swamp. McClellan met with some of his commanders at the nearby Glendale intersection early in the day and issued broad orders to defend the crossroads until all the trains, artillery, and the remainder of the army had passed. The commanding general scattered seven divisions around in a four-mile arc to cover Glendale, then left the field, riding southward to the James and then taking a cutter out to the gunboat *Galena*, where he would spend the rest of the day and part of the next. Many in the army later felt McClellan had abandoned them. The general claimed he intended to use the gunboat to scout the river and find a safe haven for his army, but he had already assigned that task to army engineers, and, in any event, it would seem that the commanding general's presence would be of greater value with his men while they awaited the approach of the enemy. McClellan had issued no specific orders to any of his generals at Glendale and had assigned none of them to overall command in his absence. "Bull" Sumner was again in command by default, and the fight that day would be a clumsy, uncoordinated effort to stave off repeated Confederate thrusts.

Stonewall Jackson at last crossed the

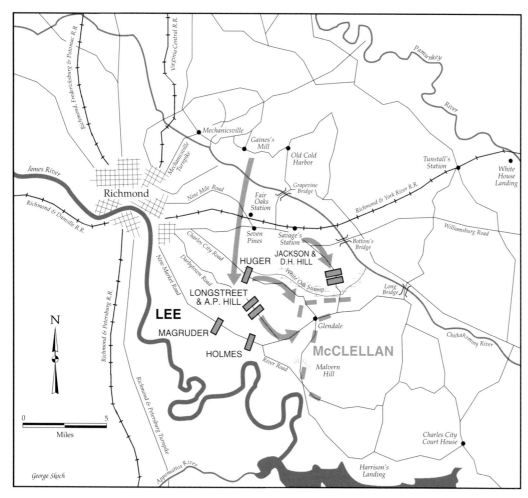

TROOP MOVEMENTS
JUNE 28–30
Following the Confederate victory at Gaines's Mill, McClellan ordered his entire army away from the Chicka-hominy and toward the James. Lee quickly recognized the oppor-tunity for cutting off McClellan's retreat and defeating the widely scattered Union forces. His plans called for a concentration of troops at the cross-roads near Glendale. On June 29 Confed-erate columns, following different routes, marched toward the cross-roads. The Union army found itself in a precarious position, with soldiers scat-tered over ten miles from the bridge at White Oak Swamp to the River Road lead-ing to Harrison's Landing.

Chickahominy early on the morning of June 30 and moved through Savage's Station, where Lee ordered him to contin-ue pursuing the Federals by way of the bridge over White Oak Swamp. The Valley general set off at once and with his more than 20,000 men made it to the swamp a little before noon, finding the bridge destroyed and the Federals in strength on the south bank. Jackson immediately deployed his artillery under cover of woods then opened a ter-rific bombardment, the size and sud-denness of which created havoc for the Federals.

"It was as if a nest of earthquakes had suddenly exploded under our feet," wrote a Vermont soldier. Terrified men, horses, and mules dashed about in confusion. The Federals arranged a few batteries to respond and the affair settled into an artillery duel in which neither side had a clear view of the other because of smoke and trees. Jackson permitted the exchange to continue all day as his caval-ry and ambitious subordinate officers probed for ways to get across the swamp. Jackson appears to have made no reason-

STONEWALL JACKSON'S
CONFEDERATES RAN
INTO STIFF RESISTANCE
AT WHITE OAK SWAMP
BRIDGE. POWERFUL
UNION ARTILLERY
BOUGHT EXTRA TIME
FOR MCCLELLAN'S
RETREAT AND THE
DEFENDERS AT
GLENDALE.
(BL)

GLENDALE OR FRAYSER'S FARM?

Having multiple names for the same battle remains one of the war's more interesting curiosities. Explanations are just as varied. One old story goes, "Well, northerners and southerners couldn't agree on much, so why should they agree on what to name the battles." Whatever the reason, this habit, popularized at Bull Run or Manassas, continued indiscriminately throughout the war.

The 1862 actions before Richmond certainly lived up to the tradition with the likes of Seven Pines (Fair Oaks), Oak Grove (King's School House), Beaver Dam Creek (Mechanicsville), and Gaines's Mill (Cold Harbor) making their way into the correspondence.

But no battle of the war goes by more names than the one fought on June 30, 1862. Union reports generally referred to the action as Glendale while Confederate writers preferred Frayser's (commonly misspelled Frazier's), Farm. Those two are just the beginning.

Many think Glendale referred to a small community or the important crossroads. It was neither. Instead Glendale was the wartime home and property of the R. H. Nelson family. The Nelson farm had belonged to the Frayser family, but that was before the war began. A popular theory has it that when the soldiers asked the locals to name the fields they had fought on, many still called it "Frayser's" even

though the family had long since moved away. Regardless, both Frayser and Nelson appear frequently in soldiers' after-action accounts.

The crossroads where the Long Bridge, Charles City, and Willis Church (or Quaker) Roads came together had several names. On one corner stood Riddell's Shop, a blacksmith business, that was used repeatedly as a battlefield reference. Just as often, though, soldiers used the major roads to name the intersection. Hence many reported on June 30 as the Battle of Charles City Crossroads.

Willis Methodist Church, a battlefield landmark, also lent its name to the day's events. Then, too, many confused the nearby New Market Road with the Long Bridge Road, adding two more battle names to the list. In a perverse twist, the Whitlock farm, site of repeated attacks on June 30, rarely turns up in accounts.

The soldiers who fought over this nondescript landscape knew it by many names. Whatever the name, this now quiet country crossroads will be forever remembered for the deeds of others long ago.

THIS PERIOD SKETCH FEATURED THE BATTLEFIELD LANDMARKS WILLIS METHODIST CHURCH, WILLIS CHURCH ROAD, AND NELSON'S FARMHOUSE.

(BL)

able attempt to move his men across either by force or by stealth, and, in fact, even found occasion for an afternoon nap. Whatever the reason for Jackson's mysterious behavior at White Oak Swamp, the effect was that the Federals on the south bank conducted yet another successful rear-guard action. For the third time in the five days of Lee's offensive, Jackson's troops would not get into the day's fight.

About two miles to the west of the stalemate at White Oak Swamp, Lee's other two attacking columns—one under Benjamin Huger and a larger force composed of A. P. Hill's and Longstreet's

divisions, tried to move directly on Glendale. Huger, slowed by trees felled across the road and blocked by Federal artillery and a division of infantry under Brigadier General Henry Slocum, could make little headway on the Charles City Road. To the south, a small column on the River Road under General Theophilus H. Holmes recoiled before massed Federal artillery and fire from gunboats. As the afternoon wore on, Lee realized that his plan to interdict the Federal retreat had gone awry and that the only hope of damaging the Federals lay with Longstreet's column on the Long Bridge Road. About 4 P.M., Lee ordered

Longstreet into the fight.

Longstreet attacked with his own and A. P. Hill's men on both sides of the Long Bridge Road. In position to meet the assault were Hill's adversaries from Beaver Dam Creek and Gaines's Mill, the Pennsylvanians of George McCall's division. Hill's and McCall's men had already done more fighting that week than any other troops, and they deserved the day off, but fate threw them together on the Long Bridge Road in what would be perhaps the most savage fighting of that week of battles.

Twenty-four field guns from six batteries—New Yorkers, Pennsylvanians, and U.S. Regulars—held the crest of a shallow rise above a ravine southwest of Glendale. The artillery presented a formidable front, made even more fearsome by McCall's 6,000 men and Phil Kearny's 7,500 infantrymen. Nearby in reserve stood two more divisions of Federal infantry under Sam Heintzelman and Sumner, plus several batteries. But Longstreet's men seemed possessed by a powerful determination and lunged for-

ward with almost irresistible recklessness. "But a single idea seemed to control the minds of the men," wrote Brigadier General James L. Kemper of his brigade's advance, "which was to reach the enemy's line by the directest route and in the shortest time; and no earthly power could have availed to arrest or restrain the impetuousity with which they rushed toward the foe."

Kemper's Virginians shattered McCall's left flank, then had to withdraw because supports did not come forward quickly enough. But McCall's line had

Lee's plan to concentrate the army and control the vital crossroads near Glendale never materialized. Stonewall Jackson's advance stalled at White Oak Swamp against two Union divisions. They spent the day exchanging artillery fire. Artillery and felled trees blocked Benjamin Huger's march along the Charles City Road. Major General Holmes provided scant support along the River Road. Only the divisions of James Longstreet and A. P. Hill reached the battlefield. Once there they met stubborn resistance from five Union divisions. In a bitter, sometimes hand-to-hand, struggle men fought one another with clubbed muskets and bayonets. Darkness brought the action to a close. The road to the James remained open.

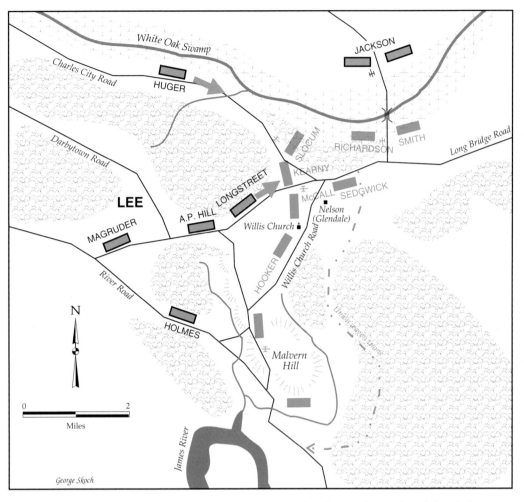

been broken and would never quite be restored in the seesaw fighting through the rest of the afternoon. Longstreet's six brigades and Hill's six repeatedly charged against McCall and Kearny, occasionally breached McCall's line, then reeled back under the force of counterattacks. The climax of the fighting came near sunset when Alabamians under Brigadier General Cadmus M. Wilcox captured the six-gun battery of Lieutenant Alanson Randol on the Long Bridge Road. The Pennsylvanians, joined by an enraged Randol and his gunners, counterattacked and retook the guns in more hand-to-hand fighting. But Virginians under Brigadier General Charles W. Field took the battery back and held it. General McCall, wounded but still riding through the darkening forest to shore up his lines,

wandered into the ranks of the 47th Virginia and went to Richmond the next day as a prisoner. McCall's survivors and their supports helped Kearny's stalwart veterans hold the line until the Confederates ceased their attacks well after 9 P.M.

Soldiers remembered the fighting at Glendale for its savagery. "No more desperate encounter took place in the war," wrote Confederate E. P. Alexander, "and nowhere else, to my knowledge, so much actual personal fighting with bayonet and butt of gun." The Federals had spent some 2,800 men in defending the army's retreat route. The Confederates had expended 3,600 in their failed attempt (which they referred to as the Battle of Frayser's Farm) to cut the Army of the Potomac to pieces.

THE FEDERAL PERSPECTIVE AT GLENDALE

Some of the most ferocious fighting of the campaign occurred on June 30 at Glendale (Frayser's Farm). The 7th Pennsylvania Reserves were in the thickest of the action. This excerpt is from a postwar account by a member of that regiment, describing an early phase of the battle.

Suddenly a Confederate regiment . . . charged in mass from the black jacks at [the] lower end of the pines, crossing the "breast works" which we had so hastily constructed and from which we had been ordered rearward. They move on a run across Randall's muzzles as though to pass round to his left. But Captain Cooper's battery is on the left of the regulars, Randall's men cease their shell fire at first sight of the charging column, quickly depress their muzzles, load grape and canister, and "let go."

The merciless guns roar in quick succession, and the carnage . . . has begun. Oh that terrible afternoon of June 30, 1862. 'Tis always foremost in my memory of the seven days' battle. The enemy is within easy musket range, and fires a few shots directed on the battery, which seemed like kicking against a whirlwind, or trying

to stop a mountain torrent. Many of them are seen to fall in the clouds of dust being raised by the grape shot striking the parched ground . . . . As we looked upon them and waited for some word of command it seemed they did not know what to do about it, that they were in the wrong place and disliked the idea of "getting out." Our gunners slammed into them with rapidity. The ground was somewhat depressed on the battery front, and in order that the canister might produce more havoc the muzzles were held well down, thus lifting the gun wheels from the ground at every discharge.

Col. Harvey commanded "Charge, seventh regiment." We moved away in almost solid mass . . . . As we advance, sounding the charge yell, we see the enemy surging slightly, but heavily, as a mighty wave, the deadly fire of the artillery still pouring into them. They seem, so to speak, to find their level, somewhat after the manner of a large body of water suddenly shot into a reservoir or other inclosure, then suddenly move as water that has found a large outlet, back by the way they had advanced . . . .

The artillery slewed their guns to the right to follow the

enemy as we made way for them, until they now fired into the pines . . . . the canister, at every discharge, barked the trees, smacking off patches as large as one's hand from two to six feet from the ground, thus suddenly exposing the white wood, reminding one of the illuminings of numerous very large fire bugs on the tree trunks . . . . I saw about 100 feet in rear, a young pine some thirty feet tall, knocked off by our canister about five feet from the ground, the trunk being carried suddenly forward and upward. The tree fell on its top; the stem pointing upward for an instant then falling over.

Holmes Alexander
Hummelstown (Pa.)
Sun, 1894

EARLY FIGHTING AT GLENDALE CENTERED ON THE CHARLES CITY ROAD. THE STRAW HATS WORN BY THE 16TH NEW YORK INFANTRY CAUGHT ONE ARTIST'S EYE.

(*BL*)

THE CAPTURE OF RANDOL'S UNION BATTERY EPITOMIZED THE CLOSE-QUARTERS FIGHTING AT GLENDALE.

(*BL*)

On the morning of July 1, 1862, Lee knew he was about out of time. McClellan's army was already on the banks of the James. If any chance to damage the Federals remained, that chance would have to be seized today. Malvern Hill was a narrow plateau of cleared land planted mostly in wheat. After months in the forests and swamps around the Chickahominy, the Northerners felt a sort of elation to be on high ground bathed in warm sunshine. "Gazing

*McClellan's forces
spread themselves
out in a U-shaped
defense, with front
lines defended by
more than two
dozen cannon. It
was, many partici-
pants later said, the
strongest position
held by either army
during the war.
After a morning of
little action, a
series of confusing
events prompted a
Confederate assault.
Lee's men were
forced to cross open
fields and climb
steep slopes before
reaching the enemy's
line. All the while
Union cannoneers
fired on the Confed-
erate ranks with
cruel efficiency.
Only darkness
ended the frightful
slaughter.*

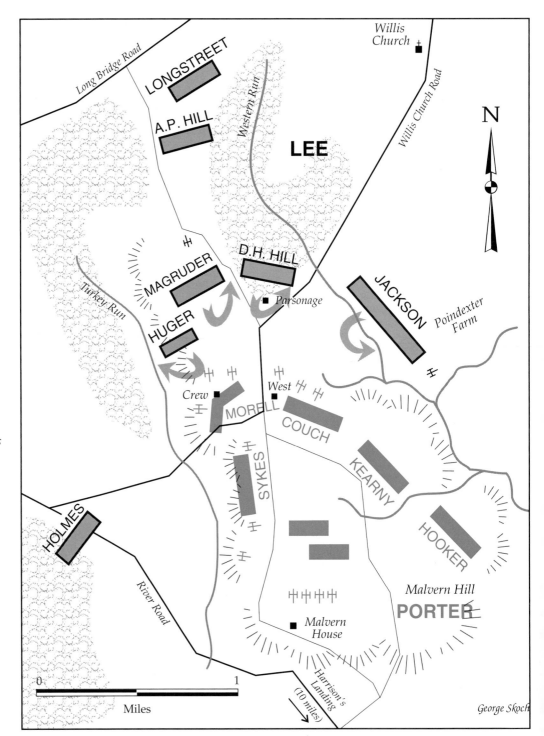

George Skoch

out over the sea of waving grain," wrote
one New Yorker, "rippling beneath the
touch of each passing breeze up to the
very breast of the high forest wall, whose
dark green foliage formed a fitting back-
ground to the picture, one could not help
being entranced. The sky, so high above,
and so blue, was flecked with light,
fleecy, silvery-white clouds, which cast

soft shadows upon the scene below, . . .
growing wheat, beneath the rays of the
declining sun, undulated and shone like
a sea of liquid gold."

McClellan's engineers, of course, had
selected the position not for its beauty but
for its defensive strength. Steep slopes on
the west, south, and east offered protection to the army's flanks and rear, so the

Federals prepared to defend the long, open northern approach—the direction from which Lee's men would come. McClellan and his officers arranged their cannon in long lines at the crest of Malvern Hill, and the guns, with the 18,000 men of George Morell's and Darius Couch's divisions in support, completely dominated the fields of wheat between them and the Confederates. The rest of the Army of the Potomac reposed nearby on the hill, waiting in support of Morell and Couch. In addition to the artillery and infantry on Malvern Hill, U.S. Navy gunboats in the James River, a little over a mile to the south, would be able to lob their enormous heavy projectiles into the ranks of Confederate attackers. The Federal position seemed impregnable.

Jackson's men, in their assigned

place on time for the first time that week, formed Lee's left flank, stretching around the northern and northeastern approaches to Malvern Hill. D. H. Hill's troops were in position in the Confederate center on the Willis Church and Carter's Mill Roads. John Magruder's guides had misled him on the morning's march and his men did not find their way to the battlefield until late in the afternoon. They formed Lee's right, facing a narrow causeway between the Carter's Mill Road and Malvern's steep western slopes.

While Lee waited for Magruder's troops to arrive, he discussed the day's prospects with Longstreet, D. H. Hill, and Jackson. Hill recognized the great strength of the Federal position and stated flatly, "If General McClellan is there in strength, we had better let him alone." Longstreet

THE OPEN GROUND AT MALVERN HILL. GENERAL PORTER'S ARTILLERY CROWNED THE DISTANT RIDGE-LINE. CONFEDERATE ASSAULTS CROSSED HERE BUT COULD ADVANCE NO FARTHER THAN THE CABINS IN THE CENTER OF THE VIEW.

(BL)

POWERFUL FEDERAL BATTERIES—SKILLFULLY OPERATED BY MEN LIKE THESE MASSACHUSETTS ARTILLERISTS— DOMINATED THE SLOPES OF MALVERN HILL.

(USAMHI)

felt differently, however, and chided Hill, "Don't get scared, now that we have got him whipped." Longstreet, though ignorant of the terrain, urged an attack. Lee agreed in principle but wished to reconnoiter the Federal position before making a decision. He found a fine artillery position on Jackson's front, and Longstreet discovered a long ridge suitable for batteries on the army's right. The two generals thought that massing Confederate guns on these two elevations would produce a converging fire on the Federal guns. The crossfire, they hoped, would weaken the Federals enough for a Confederate infantry assault to succeed. Having designed the plan of the day's action and issued the orders, Lee refrained from directing the actual operations. He was ill and though he remained on the field, he left management of the battle largely to his subordinates.

But the plan began to go wrong almost immediately. The Confederate artillery was so dispersed through the column stretching back toward Glendale that commanders could not get enough guns forward to the positions selected by Lee and Longstreet, and the bombardment never materialized. The few Southern batteries that did get into action were

knocked to pieces in minutes by the Federal gunners.

The tragedy continued when the staff officer who wrote out Lee's orders for the attack produced a badly written paper that would add to the confusion of the afternoon. Brigadier General Lewis A. Armistead's brigade of Huger's division was to trigger the assault by observing the effects of the artillery bombardment and, at what he judged the most propitious time, lead his brigade forward "with a yell." The cheering of Armistead's men would signal other commands to come forward and join the assault. Unfortunately, some of Armistead's Virginians went forward prematurely and set off a larger, badly timed advance of Confederate infantry. Magruder ordered two more brigades—those of Ambrose R. Wright and William Mahone—to support Armistead's Virginians.

The Northern artillerymen responded with a thunderous discharge of case shot and canister. Federal sharpshooters and the infantrymen of Morell and Couch laid down a steady musket fire, and the gunboats in the river added their enormous shells for good measure, though the Navy gunners' fire was inaccurate and certainly more frightening than destructive.

D. H. Hill sent his men forward in support of Magruder, but his assault lacked coordination. Though Hill had about 8,000 men available to him, he did not send them forward en masse, and the Federals were able to beat back each of the small attacks as they came. Still, wave after wave of Confederates moved out of the woods—"grim and silent as destiny itself," thought one Federal—and into the carnage in the wheat. "We have seen some grand sights," a watching Northerner wrote after the war, "some glorious and sublime spectacles in our day—but never have we beheld anything to compare in sublimity and grandeur with the scene upon which our eyes rested as column after column marched into view."

And rarely in American history had as many men fallen killed and maimed as quickly as were D. H. Hill's infantrymen cut down that afternoon. "Within fifteen or twenty minutes," wrote brigade commander Colonel John B. Gordon, "the centre regiment (Third Alabama), with which I moved, had left more than half of its number dead and wounded along its track, and the other regiments had suffered almost as severely. One shell had killed six or seven men in my immediate presence. My pistol, on one side, had the handle torn off; my canteen, on the other, was pierced, emptying its contents; my coat was ruined by having a portion of the front torn away."

The Confederates were relentless in pressing their attacks; brigade after brigade strode out of the woods, over the field littered with bodies and debris, and up the slope. For all the tremendous volume of fire from the Federal artillery,

determined Southerners under Brigadier General Lafayette McLaws fought their way all the way to the crest. "The battle was desperately contested," recalled Union artillery commander Colonel Henry Hunt, "and frequently trembled in the balance." At least one battery withdrew, and the Federal infantry found themselves hard-pressed. Fitz John Porter, who commanded the defense of Malvern Hill, for McClellan was inexplicably absent from the front for much of the day, scrambled to meet the threat. Brigades from the rear rushed forward to reinforce Morell and Couch, restored equilibrium, and drove the Confederates back with heavy loss.

The killing finally stopped just after dark, and the battlefield presented a revolting sight. Hundreds of men lay dead or dying and thousands more writhed in

UNION SKIRMISHERS, INCLUDING MEN FROM BERDAN'S SHARPSHOOTERS, PEPPERED THE CONFEDERATE POSITIONS BEFORE THE GRAND ASSAULT ON JULY 1.

(BL)

AS THE SUN SET, UNION GUNNERS CONTINUED TO BLAST THE CONFEDERATE INFANTRY ASSAULTS AGAINST THE WESTERN FACE OF MALVERN HILL.

(LC)

agony from wounds, giving the field, a Union cavalry officer thought, "a gruesome crawling appearance." The New Yorker who hours before had been entranced by the beauty of the wheat and sky wrote, "The golden sea has vanished . . . . The ground is crimson now."

With the advantages of position and plentiful artillery, the Federals still lost more than 3,000 men at Malvern Hill, but the Confederates, with few advantages at all, suffered more than 5,000 casualties. A Northerner, writing about the battle after the war, thought "the grand charge of the Confederates at Malvern is worthy of more than passing notice; it is worthy, as an exhibition of manly daring, of immortality." But D. H. Hill, less concerned with glory, saw that Malvern Hill was nothing but a terribly expensive defeat. Angry about the chaos and mismanagement that had cost so many Southern lives, Hill recorded for posterity his own judgment on Malvern Hill. "It was not war," he wrote bitterly, "It was murder."

The next day, July 2, McClellan retreated from his strong position at Malvern Hill and moved his army through a rainstorm to Berkeley and Westover Plantations on the James River. Supply officers had already begun arrangements to feed the army from Harrison's Landing at Berkeley. Lee pursued, but he and his officers decided they could do no more damage to the invaders.

So ended a week of combat that would be known at the Seven Days' Battles. At the cost of nearly 20,000 casualties, Lee had delivered Richmond from immediate danger, but the Army of the Potomac, ensconced at last on the James in a strong position under the protection of the heavy artillery of the Federal gunboats, had survived to fight another day.

But how soon would that day come? Though several of his officers urged him to take the offensive and march on Richmond, McClellan was reluctant to do so until he was heavily reinforced. He had lost some 15,000 men that week. "Little Mac" assured Washington that he was ready to resume the offensive as soon as he had enough men to do so. Lincoln visited the army at Harrison's Landing and was pleased to learn that it was not demoralized (although sickness was widespread and disease continued to cost the army thousands of men). Washington sent McClellan small numbers of reinforcements in July, but the general insisted he needed many thousands more to contend with what he believed was the Confederates' overwhelming numerical advantage. Newly appointed General in Chief Henry W. Halleck conferred with the army commander on the James and explained that the North simply did not have enough soldiers to give McClellan all the men he desired. McClellan agreed to push the campaign forward with what was available, but a few days later he resumed his pleas for more and more men. Lincoln, his patience exhausted, declared that if he could do the impossible and send McClellan 100,000 reinforcements, the general would only ask for 400,000 more. Halleck ordered the general to pack up his army and return with it to northern Virginia. The Federals began taking steamers back up the Chesepeake, and by mid-August the Peninsula campaign was over.

The Peninsula campaign was the largest, most complicated and expensive campaign of the Civil War, and that it should end in failure after so much time, money, and so many lives had been invested in its success was a source of great frustration, even embarrassment, for the Lincoln administration. The president and the War Department began making war plans that did not include McClellan, transferring most of "Little Mac's" troops to another command and removing his authority over troops in the field. The Federal disaster at Second Manassas in August 1862 moved Lincoln reluctantly to reinstate McClellan, but the general's star never again regained the luster that had so brightened Union hopes before the Peninsula campaign. In November 1862, McClellan was relieved of command and sent out of the war for good.

Much of the criticism leveled at McClellan stems from his failure to win battles. He habitually absented himself from his army's battlefields and showed none of the aggressiveness required of a

great captain. After the war, a private who had fought on the Peninsula passed judgment on his former commander and seemed to capture the essence of the McClellan era of the war in the East.

"Southern generals who fought against McClellan have said that they feared him more than any other general who commanded the Army of the Potomac, and that he struck them harder blows. This is probably correct; but it was due to the fact that the rank and file of the Army of the Potomac loved McClellan more than they loved any other commander, not even excepting Grant. Had McClellan possessed half of Grant's will and willingness to fight he would have finished up the war like a clap of thunder. Grant did not know how to retreat;

PRESIDENT ABRAHAM LINCOLN REVIEWING THE SURVIVORS OF THE ARMY OF THE POTOMAC AT HARRISON'S LANDING.

(LC)

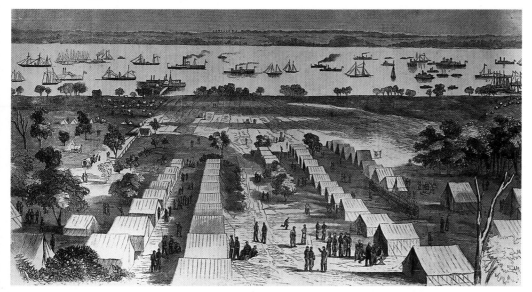

WITH NAVAL SUPPORT, THE UNION ARMY ON THE LITTLE PENINSULA AT HARRISON'S LANDING ENJOYED AN IMPREGNABLE POSITION.

(LC)

McClellan did not know how to fight. There was always a lion in his path."

One of the generals who rated McClellan highly and suffered hard blows by him was Robert E. Lee, so there is irony in that Lee contributed so heavily to the ruin of McClellan's fortunes on the Peninsula. Lee was disappointed with the result of his first campaign in command of the Army of Northern Virginia—"Under ordinary circumstances," he wrote in his report, "the enemy should have been destroyed"—but history need not share Lee's disappointment. When he took command of the army on June 1, the Confederacy stood on the precipice of defeat. Less than 30 days later, Lee had so altered the situation that his men were maneuvering for the Federal jugular, and the Army of the Potomac was fighting for its life at Glendale. It was Lee, not any other man in the Confederacy, who put the army on the offensive, directed the aggressive effort to push McClellan back from Richmond, and attempted the destruction of his army. Lee, in the right place at the right time, was the key ingredient in the Confederate renaissance in Virginia in 1862.

For almost three more years, Lee would lead his army across Virginia,

Maryland, and Pennsylvania, compiling a record of military achievement unmatched by any American soldier. The Virginian's talents as a strategist, his ability to inspire his troops to exceptional efforts, and his often untempered audacity earned him an international reputation as one of history's great generals, and nowhere did Lee's exceptional gifts flower more handsomely than amid the dismal swamps of the Chickahominy during the battles for Richmond in 1862.